A little course in...

Crochet

A little course in...

Crochet

LONDON, NEW YORK, MUNICH, MELBOURNE, DELHI

Project Editor Shashwati Tia Sarkar
Senior Art Editor Alison Shackleton
Managing Editor Penny Warren
Senior Jacket Creative Nicola Powling
Jacket Designer Rosie Levine
Senior Pre-production Producer Tony Phipps
Senior Producer Alex Bell
Art Director Jane Bull
Publisher Mary Ling

DK India
Editor Ligi John
Assistant Editor Neha Ruth Samuel
Senior Art Editor Ira Sharma
Art Editor Anjan Dey
Assistant Art Editor Pallavi Kapur
Managing Editor Alicia Ingty
Managing Art Editor Navidita Thapa
Pre-production Manager Sunil Sharma
DTP Designers Rajdeep Singh, Anurag Trivedi

Consultant Susie Johns

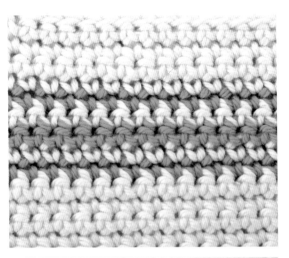

Contains some material first published in Great Britain in
Crochet Step by Step (2013), also published by Dorling Kindersley.

First published in Great Britain in 2014 by
Dorling Kindersley Limited, 80 Strand, London WC2R 0RL
Penguin Random House (UK)

6 8 10 9 7
006–196193–Jan/2014

A CIP catalogue record for this book is available
from the British Library.

ISBN 978-1-4093-3981-6

Printed and bound by Leo Paper Products Ltd, China

Discover more at
www.dk.com/crafts

Contents

1 Start Simple

2 Build On It

3 Take It Further

Build Your Course

This book is divided into three sections: Start Simple, Build On It, and Take It Further. These chapters are carefully structured to help you learn new skills and techniques and then practise your increasing knowledge by completing the step-by-step projects.

Getting Started

Going to buy your first crochet supplies can seem daunting, which is why the introduction to this book explains all you need to know about choosing a crochet hook and yarn. You will learn how the thickness of yarn and size of hook affects your finished crochet, how to match hooks to yarn, and what other equipment you might need.

Key Techniques

Close up images show you exactly what you need to do

Step-by-step photography makes it easy to for you to complete the technique

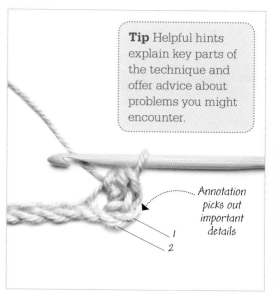

Tip Helpful hints explain key parts of the technique and offer advice about problems you might encounter.

Annotation picks out important details

The key techniques show you everything you need to know to complete your crochet projects successfully, and appear immediately before the projects they are needed for. They range from simple skills such as holding the hook and yarn, to advanced techniques such as creating intricate textures and reading colour patterns. Step-by-step photography, detailed annotation, and useful tips help you learn the skills before you attempt a project.

Patterns

Crochet patterns are stitch-by-stitch guides to making projects, stitch patterns, and motifs. Your familiarity with stitch terms will grow as you learn, and you will also learn to read crochet symbols.

Button Flower

... Pictures of the finished item show you what to aim for

Refer to the chart on pp.22–23 to remind yourself of crochet terms ...

... Crochet symbol diagrams show the pattern as an illustration. Learn about symbols on pp.124–125.

Note: cluster (cl) = (yrh twice and insert hook in sp, yrh and draw a loop through, [yrh and draw through first 2 loops on hook] twice) 4 times all in same sp (5 loops now on hook), yrh and draw through all 5 loops now on hook. This flower is worked in 2 colours (A, B).
With yarn A, make 4 ch and join with a ss to first ch to form a ring.
Round 1 (RS) 4 ch (counts as first dtr), 20 dtr in ring, join with a ss to 4th of 4-ch. Fasten off A.

Round 2 With yarn B, join with a ss to same place as last ss, 1 ch (does not count as a st), 1 dc in same place as last ss, (5 ch, miss next 2 dtr, 1 dc in next dtr) 6 times, 5 ch, join with a ss to first dc of round.
Round 3 * (1 ss, 4 ch, 1 cluster, 4 ch, 1 ss) in next 5-ch loop; rep from * 6 times more, join with a ss to same place as last ss in round 2.
Fasten off.
Sew a small button on to the centre of the flower.

The perfect **Project**

To help you achieve the best possible result, its design, construction, and the techniques involved, are discussed in detail.

Annotation highlights key stitchings and other details ...

Trickier parts of the pattern are analysed ...

... Seams and methods of construction are flagged up

Key **Details**

These useful illustrated boxes pick out the defining features of your project and explain how to achieve them with extra advice and tips.

Essential **Equipment**

CROCHET HOOKS

When you are beginning to learn crochet, start with a good-quality standard metal crochet hook. Once you know how to work the basic stitches with a lightweight yarn (see p.17) and a 4mm or 4.5mm (US size 6 or 7) hook, branch out and try some other types of hooks in order to find the one that suits you best.

Parts of a crochet hook

The hook lip grabs the yarn to form the loops and the shank determines the size of the loop. The crochet handle gives weight to the tool and provides a good grip.

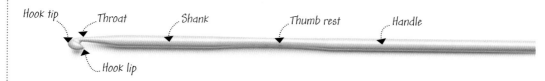

Hook tip · · · Throat · · Shank · · Thumb rest · · Handle

· · · Hook lip

Hook types

Metal hooks
Aluminium hooks are smooth and move easily through loops of yarn, making them a great choice for beginners. Bright colours are available as well as the standard grey.

Wooden hooks
Hardwood and bamboo hooks are attractive and lighter in weight than metal hooks. The hook lips are not always as smooth, however, and can catch on the yarn, so wait until you are comfortable with crochet stitches before trying a wooden hook.

Plastic hooks
Plastic hooks are not as durable or as precisely made as metal and wooden hooks, but they are light in weight, so are enjoyable to work with.

Jumbo hooks
The largest crochet hook sizes – from a 10mm (US size N-15) to a 20mm (US size S) are made in plastic to keep them light. They are used for making thick crochet fabric very quickly.

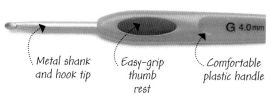

Metal shank and hook tip · Easy-grip thumb rest · Comfortable plastic handle

Comfort handle
Hook handles come in different shapes. If you find the standard crochet hook uncomfortable to hold because it is too narrow, investigate hooks with alternative handles. This example is designed and refined especially for comfort and good grip.

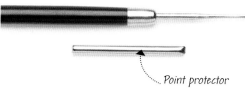

Point protector

Lace hook
Because lace crochet hooks are so fine, ranging from 0.6mm (US size 14 steel) to 1.75mm (US size 5 steel), they are always manufactured in metal to prevent them from snapping. Store them with their metal point protectors in place to avoid accidents.

Hook sizes
Crochet hooks are manufactured in the various sizes (diameters) listed in the hook conversion chart on the right. The millimetre sizes are the diameters of the hook shank, which determine the size of the crochet stitches.

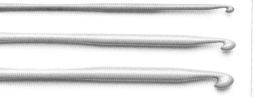

Although the middle range of hook sizes – from 2mm (US size B-1) to 9mm (US size M-13) – are the most commonly used, the finer hooks are used for lace crochet and the thicker hooks are popular for jumbo crochet. See page 17 for which hook size to use with the different yarn weights.

Conversion chart

This chart gives the conversions between the various hook-size systems. Where there are no exact conversions available, use the nearest equivalent.

Metric	US Sizes	Old UK
0.6mm	14 steel	
0.75mm	12 steel	
1mm	11 steel	
1.25mm	7 steel	
1.5mm	6 steel	
1.75mm	5 steel	
2mm		14
2.25mm	B-1	
2.5mm		12
2.75mm	C-2	
3mm		10
3.25mm	D-3	
3.5mm	E-4	9
3.75mm	F-5	
4mm	G-6	8
4.5mm	7	7
5mm	H-8	6
5.5mm	I-9	5
6mm	J-10	4
6.5mm	K-10½	3
7mm		2
8mm	L-11	
9mm	M-13	
10mm	N-15	
12mm	P	
15mm	Q (16mm)	
20mm	S (19mm)	

NATURAL FIBRES

Yarns can be made from all sorts of fibres and, in theory, you can crochet with any yarn. Each type of fibre has its own attributes, though, that should be considered when choosing an appropriate yarn for your project. Fibres sourced from nature, such as animal hair and plant fibre, are popular for their appealing, breathable textures, but they can be more expensive than yarns with synthetic fibre content.

Cotton

Cotton yarns are very popular for crochet because their smooth texture gives good stitch definition, showing intricate patterns clearly. This plant fibre is breathable and light, but also robust, easy to wash, and doesn't shed fibres easily, making it great for homewares, gadget covers, and bags. A lightweight (above left) or fine cotton yarn (above right) is best for practising crochet techniques. See pages 17–19 for more about yarn weights.

Mercerized cotton

Cotton fibre is sometimes mercerized, a process that compresses it and transforms it into an ultra-strong yarn with a reflective sheen. Mercerized cotton is a good choice for a project that needs to be strong and hold its shape, such as a clutch bag (see pp.122–123), a summer cardigan, or a throw.

Cotton crochet thread

Crochet was traditionally worked using cotton threads to make an alternative to bobbin and needle lace. Today, cotton threads are still used for decorative lace edgings and filet crochet (see pp.168–173 and pp.139–141).

Silk

The silkworm spins a cocoon in order to develop into a moth and it is from these fibres that silk is made. Silk has a shiny, sleek appearance and a luxurious texture but it is expensive to buy. Yarns containing silk blended with other fibres are more affordable and are perfect for baby clothes and special-occasion wear.

Wool

Sheep's fleeces produce very warm, hard-wearing yarns, whether they are pure wool or blended with other fibres. Some wool fibres can be quite rough, but will soften with wear. Wool is ideal for warm blankets, hats, and gloves but can shrink with washing.

Alpaca

A relative of the llama, the alpaca provides one of the warmest natural fibres with a soft, luxurious, slightly fuzzy feel. Alpaca yarns are perfect for winter items, but they don't offer precise stitch definition like cotton or silk, and will give a softer look.

Cashmere

This fibre is spun from the hair of a goat, and makes an ultra-luxurious, velvety-soft yarn. Cashmere is expensive to produce and so it is often blended with other fibres to lend its softness to more affordable yarns. Enjoy cashmere close to the skin with crocheted scarves, snoods, or jumpers. Many cashmere yarns are dry-clean only.

SYNTHETIC FIBRES AND YARN BLENDS

Yarns spun from man-made fibres offer strength, washability, and affordability, if not the insulating properties and softness of natural fibres. For this reason, they are often included in yarn blends to combine their attributes with those of other fibres.

Nylon

Polyamide, or nylon, is an incredibly strong and lightweight fibre. Its elasticity is often used to reinforce yarn blends. Like other man-made fibres, nylon improves the washability of the fibres it is blended with by preventing shrinkage and felting. It is a good choice for items that may be subjected to heavy wear.

Acrylic

Acrylic fibres are very cheap to manufacture and often come in bright and luminous shades that are hard to create with natural fibres. Acrylic yarn feels slightly rougher than other synthetics, but it is robust and resistant to moths, making it ideal for toys, novelty items, and budget projects.

Natural and synthetic mixes

Man-made fibres, such as microfibre, are often blended with natural fibres, such as wool and mohair, to bind them together and prevent shedding and reduce pilling; they also help to prevent animal fibres shrinking when washed. The strength of such blends makes them perfect for socks or gloves.

Wool and cotton mixes

Sometimes natural fibres are blended together – the strength and softness of cotton adds smoothness, breathability, and washability to wool's warm (and sometimes scratchy) qualities. Wool sheds fewer hairs when mixed with a stabilizing plant fibre, so this blend is great for babies and those with sensitive skin.

SPECIALITY YARNS

There are countless speciality yarns that offer exciting textures, colours, and finishes. Any of them can be crocheted but, as a general rule, multicoloured, heavily textured yarns are better suited to basic stitches, while smoother ones show lots of stitch detail.

Tape yarn

Also called ribbon yarn, the main characteristic of tape yarn is its flat shape. It may also be tubular, and becomes flattened when wound into a ball. Its interesting, crisp texture gives lovely stitch definition and it looks particularly good with openwork stitch patterns (see pp.146–149).

Metallic yarn

Lurex and other metallic yarns make highly effective trims and decorations. They may be uncomfortable to wear against the skin if used on their own, but if blended with other yarns, they create very interesting mixes and are fun to experiment with. Metallic yarns often come in thinner yarn weights.

Spun yarn

Very thick yarns, when loosely spun, are less dense than regular yarns, and are light and bouncy. These chunky yarns are intended to prevent finished items from feeling heavy and are ideal for crocheting bulky cardigans, blankets, and pram covers.

Plied yarn

A plied yarn is made up of two or more strands of spun fibre twisted together. Originally, the number of "plies" defined a yarn's thickness, but these days many plied yarns vary in weight and are likely to contain several colours.

UNUSUAL YARNS

*These unusual yarns are great fun to experiment with. Some stiffer materials,
such as thick wire and string, can be tiring to work with, so try using them for
small projects and make sure you crochet a small swatch before you begin.*

Fabric

*Crocheting strips of fabric cut from old clothes and other
textiles into doormats and rugs is a time-honoured method
of recycling. Tie fabric strips together and wind into a ball.
Choose a hook size to suit the thickness of the strips.*

Wire

*This unusual medium is often used for crocheting jewellery:
buy beading wire and crochet it into chokers, necklaces, and
bracelets. Try stranding beads onto the wire before you work and
crochet them in place as you go along. For a really unusual
project, strand the wire with another yarn to form a malleable
fabric that can be shaped into a sculpture.*

String

*Ideal for crocheting practical household items such as
bowls and boxes, string is available in a range of colours
and weights. Experiment with a medium-sized hook,
such as 5mm (US8), to create a very stiff fabric capable
of holding its shape. Coat finished household items with
diluted PVA glue to waterproof them.*

Plastic bags

*Recycle plastic bags by cutting them into strips and joining them
together with knots to form yarn. Crochet with a large hook (10mm
(US15) upwards is recommended) to suit the width of the strips
and how tight you would like the fabric to be (see pp.18–19). Plastic
yarn is great for making bags, mats, and waterproof items such as
toiletry bags or garden seat covers.*

OTHER EQUIPMENT

Besides a hook and some yarn, crocheters need very little equipment to get started. Some scissors, blunt-ended yarn needles, and a tape measure are essential items; other equipment, such as yarn bobbins, are useful additions.

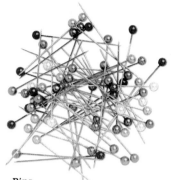

Pins
Use pins with glass heads or large heads (such as knitting pins), for seams and blocking (see p.103).

Yarn bobbins
Useful for holding short lengths of yarn for colourwork crochet (see p.153).

Row counter
These are useful for keeping track of where you are in your crochet. String on a length of cotton yarn and hang it around your neck – change it each time you complete a row.

Blunt-ended yarn needles
Use these for sewing seams and darning in yarn ends (make sure the eye of the needle is big enough for your chosen yarn).

Stitch markers
These can be hooked onto the crochet to mark a specific row, stitch, or the right side of your work. Simple safety pins make excellent markers.

Tape measure
Keep a tape measure on hand for checking your tension and measuring your crochet.

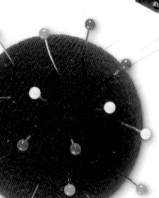

Pincushion
A useful item for storing pins safely when working.

Scissors
A sharp pair of scissors is essential for cutting yarn and trimming off yarn ends.

Buying **Yarns**

TYPES OF YARN PACKAGING

When buying yarns, you will see that they are presented in different formats. Balls and donuts of yarn can be used straight away, but hanks (often used for premium yarns) need a little preparation before you begin to crochet.

Hank

Also called a skein, a hank is a twisted ring of yarn. It needs to be wound into a ball before it can be used. This gives you the opportunity to check that there are no knots or faults in the yarn as you wind it. Many soft, delicate fibres, such as silk and spun yarns are sold as hanks.

Ball
A ball of yarn is ready to use. Pull the yarn from the centre and keep the label in place as you work to make sure that the ball doesn't totally unravel.

Donut
Some yarns are presented in a donut-like shape. Like balls, these are ready to use: just pull the yarn from the centre to start crocheting.

YARN LABELS

Everything you need to know about a yarn is on its label. It will include symbols that tell you how to crochet with it and how to launder it. Here is just a selection of the most common symbols. Always keep the labels: they are vital for identifying the yarn if you run short and need to buy more. New yarn should have the same dye lot number as the original purchase in order to avoid a slight difference in colour in the finished item.

Symbols

Yarn manufacturers may use a system of symbols to give details of a yarn. These include descriptions of suitable hooks and the required tension.

Recommended crochet hook size

Tension over a 10cm (4in) test square

Shade/colour number

Dye lot number

Fibre content

Yarn weight and thickness

Weight of ball, hank, or skein

Ballband

A yarn label is also known as a ballband. Information on the yarn's weight and thickness, as well as washing guidelines, are printed on this band. Yarns range from very fine and light to thick, dense, and heavy.

YARN WEIGHT CHART

Yarn "weight" refers to its thickness. The chart belows shows which range of hook sizes is usually recommended for each weight category of yarn. Your choice of hook will depend on the stitch tension you need for your project (see p.18).

What do You Want to Crochet?	Yarn Weight	Yarn Symbol	Recommended Hook Sizes		
			METRIC	US	OLD UK
Lace, doilies	2-ply, lace, fingering	0 Lace	1.5mm 1.75mm 2mm 2.25mm	6 steel 5 steel N/A B-1	N/A N/A 14 N/A
Babywear, shawls	3-ply, superfine, fingering, baby	1 Super fine	2.75mm 3mm 3.25mm	C-2 N/A D-3	N/A 10 N/A
Babywear, lightweight clothing, accessories	4-ply, fine, sportweight, baby	2 Fine	3.25mm 3.5mm 3.75mm	D-3 E-4 F-5	N/A 9 N/A
Clothing, lightweight scarves, blankets, toys	Double-knit (DK), light worsted, 5–6 ply	3 Light	3.75mm 4mm 4.5mm	F-5 G-6 7	N/A 8 7
Blankets, hats, thick scarves, mittens	Aran, medium, worsted, Afghan, 12-ply	4 Medium	5mm 5.5mm	H-8 I-9	6 5
Rugs, jackets, blankets, legwarmers, winter hats and accessories	Chunky, bulky, craft, rug, 14-ply	5 Bulky	6mm 6.5mm 7mm 8mm	J-10 K-10½ N/A L-11	4 3 2 N/A
Heavy blankets, rugs, very thick scarves	Super bulky, super chunky, bulky, roving, 16-ply and upwards	6 Super bulky	9mm 10mm	M-13 N-15	N/A N/A

Understanding **Tension**

"Tension" is a term that describes stitch size, and it affects how large or small your finished crochet piece will be. Tension differs depending on yarn thickness (see p.17), hook size, and how tightly or loosely you crochet (which varies from person to person). You should not attempt to amend your tension by changing how tightly you crochet, as this may produce inconsistent results. Instead, change the size of the hook, as shown below. Every swatch shown has exactly the same number of double crochet stitches.

Fine yarn tension swatches

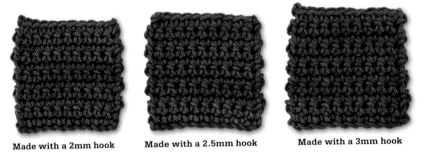

Made with a 2mm hook   Made with a 2.5mm hook   Made with a 3mm hook

The larger the hook size, the larger the swatch it creates. The difference is subtle on a small scale, but will magnify as more rows are added. This fine 4-ply yarn is the thinnest yarn weight shown here, so its swatches are the smallest.

Lightweight yarn tension swatches

Made with a 3.5mm hook   Made with a 4mm hook   Made with a 4.5mm hook

The varying tension (or scale) of the stitches in the lightweight DK yarn swatches is clearly visible as the hook size changes. The smaller hook creates a tighter, firmer fabric than the larger hook, which creates a softer, more flexible texture.

Bulky yarn tension swatches

Made with a 6mm hook   Made with a 7mm hook   Made with an 8mm hook

Each hook size creates a different stitch tension in these chunky yarn swatches. They show that any of the three hooks could be a suitable choice – it depends on the tension given in your pattern or on the effect you would like to achieve with the yarn you are using.

Checking tension

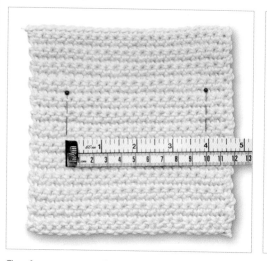

Crochet patterns describe tension in terms of the number of stitches in a given area, usually 10cm (4in) wide. For instance, the pattern may say: "17 htr to 10cm (4in)". To check that you achieve the recommended tension, make a sample of the pattern you are following and mark out the area stated in the tension guide. Count the stitches; if you have more than the recommended number you will need a larger hook size; if you have fewer stitches, use a smaller hook. See page 102 for the full technique.

Choosing Colours

YARN COLOURS

Colour affects the appearance of a finished item dramatically, so choose with care. The colour wheel – made up of all the colours in the spectrum – can be a useful tool when choosing colour combinations. Make samples to test that the colours work well together before buying large quantities of yarn.

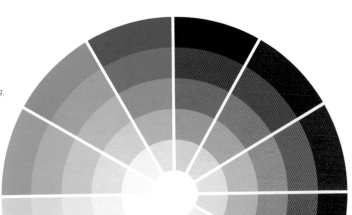

Using a colour wheel

This diagram shows how colours on opposite sides of the wheel – red and green, for example, or yellow and violet – contrast with each other and make both colours stand out, while colours that lie side by side harmonize with each other.

Black and white

Black and white do not appear on the colour wheel, since they are not classified as colours. Black yarn does not display textured stitches to best effect and can be difficult and tiring to work with, because stitches are more difficult to see. White yarns show up the subtleties of stitch patterns, but they also show up dirty marks and need washing more frequently.

Warm shades

The warm end of the spectrum encompasses reds, oranges, yellows, and red-violet. These colours provide richness as well as brightness. A blend of warm shades can be very flattering.

Pastels

Pale colours are very popular for baby clothes and also tend to feature in pattern collections for spring and summer garments. It is easy to combine a number of pastel shades harmoniously.

Brights

Vivid shades are popular for children's clothing and will appeal to crocheters who like to make a strong statement. If you are not confident about combining several bright colours, it may be easier to stick with a single colour – or try pairing two bright shades for eye-catching striped jumpers or accessories.

Cool shades

Blues, greens, and violets are at the cool end of the spectrum and tend to be darker in tone than warm shades. Hold different-coloured balls of yarn against your face to judge what suits you best.

Seasonal mixtures

The colours of nature – hues that are similar to such things as sunsets, earth tones, and leaves – are more subtle, and a popular choice for men's clothing. Combine them in multicoloured projects that feature intarsia (see p.153) or stripes.

Crochet **Abbreviations and Terms**

These charts show the most common terms and abbreviations used in crochet patterns. Some crochet terms are different in the UK and US so when following a pattern, be sure to know whether it is written in UK or US terms. This book uses UK terms.

Stitch terms and abbreviations

UK/US Abbreviation	UK term	US term
ch	chain stitch	chain stitch
ss	slip stitch	slip stitch
dc / sc	double crochet	single crochet
htr / hdc	half treble crochet	half double crochet
tr / dc	treble crochet	double crochet
dtr / tr	double treble crochet	treble crochet
trtr / dtr	triple treble crochet	double treble crochet
qtr / trtr	quadruple treble crochet	triple treble crochet
quintr / quadtr	quintuple treble crochet	quadruple treble crochet
2 dc in same st / 2 sc in same st (same abbreviation can apply to htr, tr, dtr, etc.)	1-st increase, or work two stitches into same stitch (p.90 and p.98)	1-st increase, or work two stitches into same stitch (p.90 and p.98)
3 dc in same st / 3 sc in same st (same abbreviation can apply to htr, tr, dtr, etc.)	2-st increase, or work three stitches into same stitch (p.90 and p.98)	2-st increase, or work three stitches into same stitch (p.90 and p.98)
dc2tog / sc2tog (same abbreviation can apply to htr, tr, dtr, etc.)	1-stitch decrease, or work two stitches together to merge (p.92 and p.100)	1-stitch decrease, or work two stitches together to merge (p.92 and p.100)
dc3tog / sc3tog (same abbreviation can apply to htr, tr, dtr, etc.)	2-stitch decrease, or work three stitches together to merge (p.92 and p.100)	2-stitch decrease, or work three stitches together to merge (p.92 and p.100)
fptr / fpdc	front post treble crochet (p.132)	front post double crochet (p.132)
bptr / bpdc	back post treble crochet (p.133)	back post double crochet (p.133)
2-, 3-, 4-, 5-, or 6-tr shell / 2-, 3-, 4-, 5-, or 6-dc shell	shell, made with 2, 3, 4, 5, or 6 treble crochet stitches worked into the same stitch (p.116)	shell, made with 2, 3, 4, 5, or 6 double crochet stitches worked into the same stitch (p.116)
2-, 3-, 4-, 5-, or 6-tr cluster / 2-, 3-, 4-, 5-, or 6-dc cluster	cluster, made with 2, 3, 4, 5, or 6 treble crochet stitches that are joined at the top (p.117)	cluster, made with 2, 3, 4, 5, or 6 double crochet stitches that are joined at the top (p.117)

ABBREVIATIONS AND TERMS

UK/US Abbreviation	UK term	US term
3-, 4-, 5-tr bobble / 3-, 4-, 5-dc bobble	bobble, made with 3, 4, or 5 trebles worked into the same place and joined at the top (p.118)	bobble, made with 3, 4, or 5 doubles worked into the same place and joined at the top (p.118)
3-, 4-, 5-tr popcorn / 3-, 4-, 5-dc popcorn	popcorn, a bobble variation made with 3, 4, or 5 trebles (p.119)	popcorn, a bobble variation made with 3, 4, or 5 doubles (p.119)
3-, 4-, 5-ch picot	picot, made with 3, 4, or 5 chain stitches (p.138)	picot, made with 3, 4, or 5 chain stitches (p.138)

Other terms and abbreviations

alt	alternate
beg	begin(ning)
cont	continu(e)(ing)
dec	decreas(e)(ing)
facing	facing towards you as you are working
fasten off	cut the yarn and draw it through the working loop to secure it
foll	follow(s)(ing)
foundation chain	the base of chain stitches that the first row is worked into
foundation row	the first row of crochet (the row worked into the foundation chain)
inc	increas(e)(ing)
miss / skip a stitch	do not work into the stitch, but go on to the next stitch
patt(s)	pattern(s)
rem	remain(s)(ing)
rep	repeat(s)(ing)
RS	right side
sp	space(s)
st(s)	stitch(es)
TBL	through back loop
TFL	through front loop
tog	together
turning chain	the chains worked at the beginning of the row (or round) to bring the hook up to the correct height for working the following stitches in the row (p.66)
WS	wrong side
yrh / yo	yarn round hook (yarn over in US)
*	repeat instructions after asterisk, or between asterisks, as many times as instructed

1
Start Simple

The lovely, decorative appearance of crochet may look complex, but this craft is much easier to learn than many people think. In this chapter, you will find out how to work all the basic crochet stitches and some easy stitch variations. Compared to knitting, crochet has more basic stitches for a beginner to master, but you can take your time to learn them one by one. When you feel comfortable with a stitch, have fun practising it with a simple project, such as a pretty washcloth or a practical phone cover.

Learn to crochet:

Washcloth
pp.40–41

Phone Cover
pp.50–51

Cafetière Cosy
pp.56–59

Friendship Bracelets
pp.72–75

How to **Make a Slip Knot**

Making a slip knot is always the first step when starting a piece of crochet. The knot attaches your yarn to the hook and creates the first loop; crochet is essentially done by working a hook through a series of loops. A cotton DK weight yarn and a 4.5mm hook are easy to practise with – choose a smooth yarn with a tight ply that won't split easily.

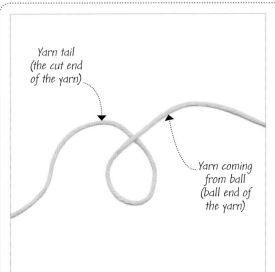

Yarn tail (the cut end of the yarn)

Yarn coming from ball (ball end of the yarn)

Tip Follow the direction of the large grey arrows to make the movement of the crochet hook.

1 To make the first loop (a slip knot) on your hook, begin by crossing the yarn coming from the ball in front of the yarn end (called the yarn tail) to form a loop of yarn.

2 Insert the tip of the hook through the loop of yarn. Then use the hook to grab the ball end of the yarn and pull the yarn through the loop towards you.

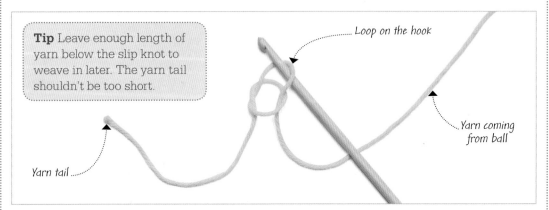

Tip Leave enough length of yarn below the slip knot to weave in later. The yarn tail shouldn't be too short.

Loop on the hook

Yarn coming from ball

Yarn tail

3 This forms a loop on the hook and a loose, open slip knot below the loop. Alternatively, you can make a slip knot with your fingers and slip the loop onto the hook.

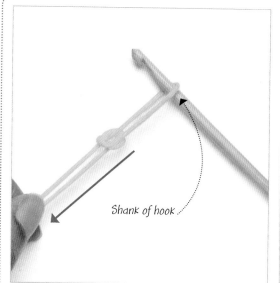

Shank of hook

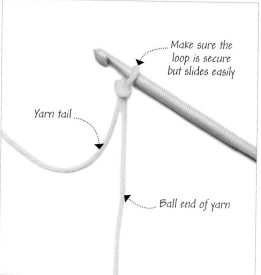

Make sure the loop is secure but slides easily

Yarn tail

Ball end of yarn

4 Pull the ends of the yarn to tighten the knot and the loop around the shank of the hook. Avoid closing the loop around the thin throat of the hook, or it will be too tight.

5 The completed slip knot should be tight enough on the hook so that it won't fall off, but not so tight that you can barely slide it along the hook's shank.

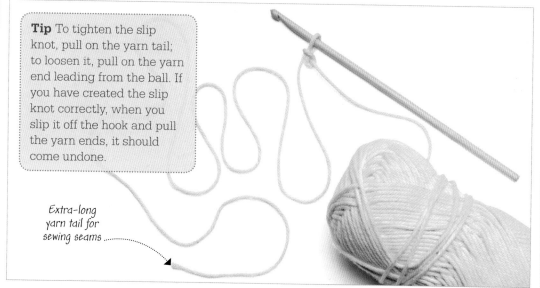

Tip To tighten the slip knot, pull on the yarn tail; to loosen it, pull on the yarn end leading from the ball. If you have created the slip knot correctly, when you slip it off the hook and pull the yarn ends, it should come undone.

Extra-long yarn tail for sewing seams

6 The yarn tail on the slip knot should be at least 10cm (4in) long so it can be threaded into a blunt-ended yarn needle and woven in later. However, a crochet pattern may instruct you to leave an extra-long yarn tail (called a long loose end) to use for seams or other purposes.

How to **Hold the Yarn and Hook**

There is no right or wrong way to hold a crochet hook and yarn. The most common methods are shown below, but any hold that feels comfortable and creates a consistent tension on the yarn is good. The hook is held in the dominant hand and the yarn is held in the other, so left-handed crocheters will be performing the mirror image of right hand examples.

Holding the yarn

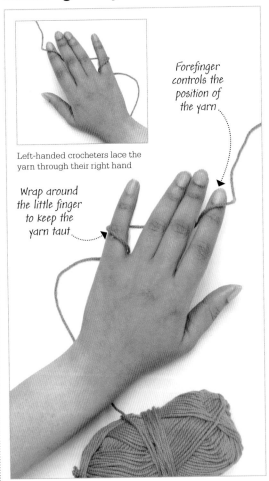

Forefinger controls the position of the yarn

Left-handed crocheters lace the yarn through their right hand

Wrap around the little finger to keep the yarn taut

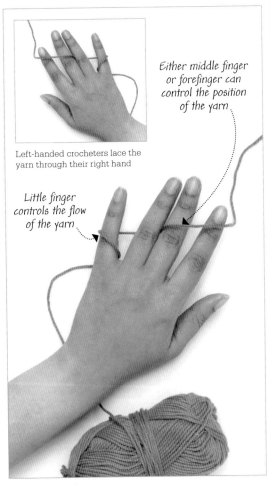

Either middle finger or forefinger can control the position of the yarn

Left-handed crocheters lace the yarn through their right hand

Little finger controls the flow of the yarn

METHOD ONE
Wind the yarn around your little finger, then pass it under your two middle fingers and over your forefinger. With this method, the forefinger is used to position the yarn.

METHOD TWO
Wrap the yarn around your little finger, pass it behind the next finger, and over the top of the remaining fingers to allow you to use either forefinger or middle finger to control the yarn.

Holding the hook

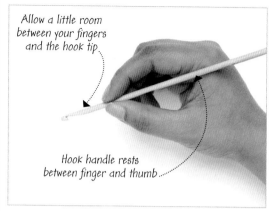

Allow a little room between your fingers and the hook tip

Hook handle rests between finger and thumb

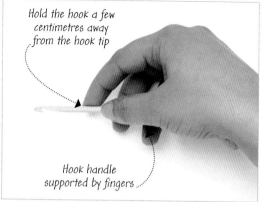

Hold the hook a few centimetres away from the hook tip

Hook handle supported by fingers

PENCIL POSITION

Hold the hook in any comfortable position. In this position, grip the crochet hook as you would a pencil, whichever hand you are using. If the hook has a shaped thumb rest (see p.8), use it to guide where to place your fingers.

KNIFE POSITION

In the knife position, grip the hook as you would when using a table knife to cut food, whichever hand you are using. Hold the hook a few centimetres from the tip, or use the thumb rest as a guide for your fingers.

Tensioning your yarn

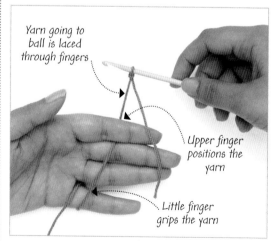

Yarn going to ball is laced through fingers

Upper finger positions the yarn

Little finger grips the yarn

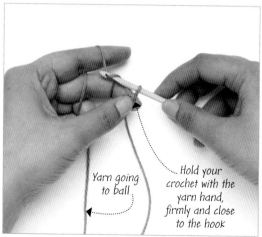

Yarn going to ball

Hold your crochet with the yarn hand, firmly and close to the hook

1 With the slip knot on your hook, lace the yarn through your fingers as desired, but so that it ends up over the tip of either your forefinger or middle finger. As you crochet, grip the yarn with your little finger.

2 With your little finger and ring finger, grip and release the yarn gently as you form the loops. Use an upper finger to position the yarn, and hold the base of the slip knot close to the hook to keep it steady.

How to **Make Chain Stitches** (Abbreviation = *ch*)

Chain stitches are the first crochet stitches to learn because they form foundation chains – the starting point for all crochet fabrics, like a "cast on" in knitting – and are also used to connect rows. Practise chain stitches until you feel comfortable holding a hook and releasing and tensioning yarn. Start with a slip knot on your hook (see p.26).

Making a foundation chain

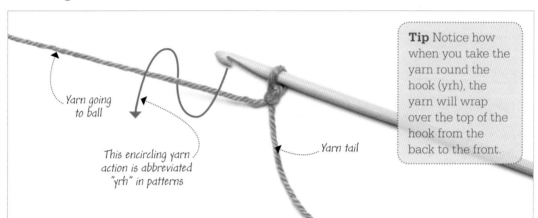

Yarn going to ball

This encircling yarn action is abbreviated "yrh" in patterns

Yarn tail

Tip Notice how when you take the yarn round the hook (yrh), the yarn will wrap over the top of the hook from the back to the front.

1 Wrap the yarn around the hook by moving your hook under the yarn while bringing the yarn slightly forwards towards you. This action is called "yarn round hook" (abbreviated to "yrh"). Hold the base of the slip knot steady with the free fingers of your yarn hand.

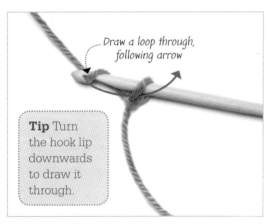

Draw a loop through, following arrow

Tip Turn the hook lip downwards to draw it through.

First chain made

2 With the yarn gripped in the lip of the hook, draw a loop of yarn through the loop on the hook. Turn the hook lip downwards to pull it through without snagging the loop.

3 This completes the first chain. Yrh and draw a loop through the loop on the hook for each new stitch. Keep your hands relaxed and try to keep an even tension on the yarn.

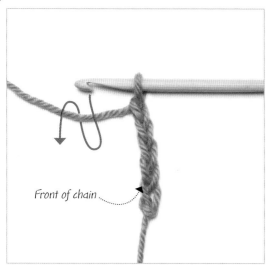

Front of chain

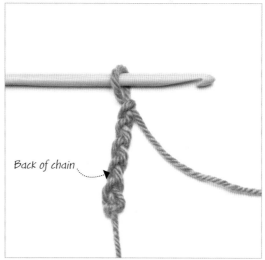

Back of chain

4 Continue making chains until you have the number specified in your crochet pattern. Don't worry if the chains aren't even the first time – practice makes perfect.

5 The chains at the front of the foundation chain form little "V" shapes. The back of the foundation chain has little bumps along it, as seen here.

Counting chain stitches

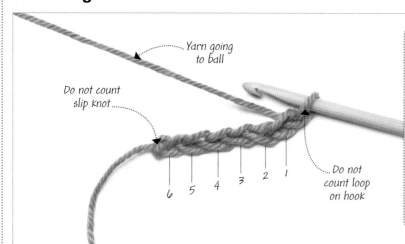

Yarn going to ball

Do not count slip knot

6 5 4 3 2 1

Do not count loop on hook

Tip It doesn't matter if you make a mistake in crochet – you can always undo it. Just remove the hook and pull the ball-end yarn to undo stitches. Start again by putting the hook back in the loop.

Before starting on the first row of your crochet fabric, check the number of chains you have made in the foundation chain. With the front of the chain facing you, count the "V" shapes – each one is a chain stitch. The loop on the hook does not count as a stitch. The slip knot can sometimes look like a "V" shape, but be careful not to count it as a stitch.

How to **Make Slip Stitches** (Abbreviation = *ss*)

Crochet stitches are often described in terms of height; as you learn the basic crochet stitches, you will notice that each one is taller than the last. Slip stitches are the shortest of all the crochet stitches. They are not worked in rows very often because they make a very dense fabric, but they are essential to learn for joining other stitches together.

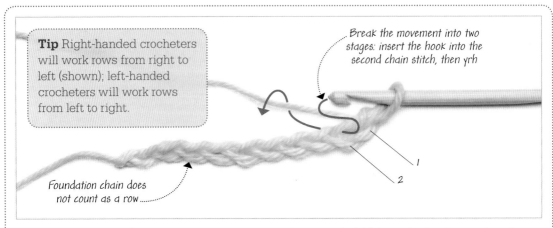

Tip Right-handed crocheters will work rows from right to left (shown); left-handed crocheters will work rows from left to right.

Break the movement into two stages: insert the hook into the second chain stitch, then yrh

Foundation chain does not count as a row

1
2

1 Make a foundation chain as long as you require. To begin the first slip stitch of the first row, insert the hook through the second chain stitch (ch) from the hook, passing the hook under only one strand of the chain. Then wrap the yarn around the hook (yrh).

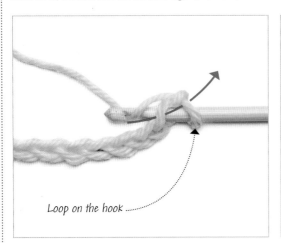

Loop on the hook

Tip Slip stitches can be tricky to work in rows because they are so tiny. Don't be discouraged!

Chain stitches will stretch as you work into them

2 Holding the base of the chain firmly with the fingers of your yarn hand and tensioning the yarn (see p.29), draw a loop back through both the chain and the loop on the hook as shown by the large arrow.

3 Continue across the foundation chain, working a slip stitch (ss) into each chain in the same way. Always work slip stitches fairly loosely; they are so short that they are difficult to work into if they are too tight.

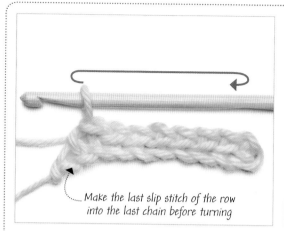

Make the last slip stitch of the row into the last chain before turning

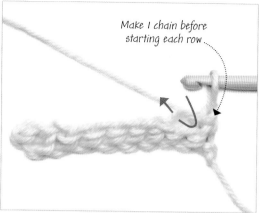

Make I chain before starting each row

4 After the last stitch of the row has been completed, turn the piece of crochet so the back is now facing you. For right-handers, the hook should now be at the right edge of the row; for left-handers it will be at the left.

5 Begin a second row by making one chain stitch. This chain is called the turning chain. For the second and following rows of slip stitch, work each ss into the top strand (called the back loop) of the stitches below.

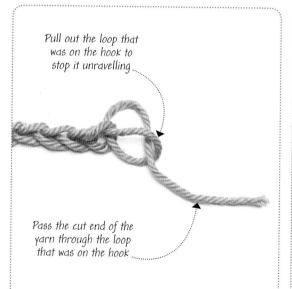

Pull out the loop that was on the hook to stop it unravelling

Pass the cut end of the yarn through the loop that was on the hook

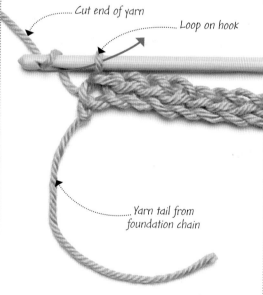

Cut end of yarn

Loop on hook

Yarn tail from foundation chain

Fastening off stitches

Remove the loop from the hook. Cut the yarn, leaving the tail long enough to weave in later. Pass the cut end of the yarn through the loop and pull tight to close.

Fastening off with a hook

Alternatively, you can use the hook to draw the cut end through the remaining loop as shown here by the large arrow. Fastening off is the same for all stitches.

How to **Work Double Crochet** (Abbreviation = *dc*)

Double crochet is the easiest crochet stitch to learn. It is a short stitch and the compact fabric it creates is really attractive and great for many types of garments and accessories, including toys and containers. Take your time learning and practising the stitch because once you become proficient, the taller stitches will be much easier to master.

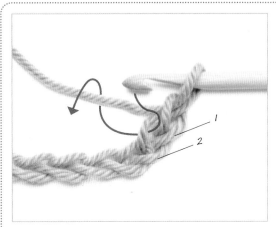

Hold the base of the
chain as you draw the
yarn through

1 Make a foundation chain as long as you require. Insert the hook through the second chain (ch) from the hook. Wrap the yarn around the hook (yrh), following the large arrow.

2 Holding the base of the chain firmly with your yarn hand and tensioning the yarn (see p.29), draw a loop back through the chain as shown by the large arrow.

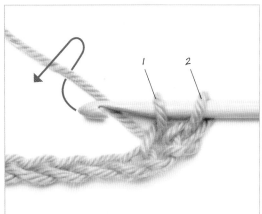

3 There are now 2 loops on the hook. Next, yrh a second time as shown by the large arrow. The foundation chain may stretch as you work into it, but this is normal.

4 Draw the yarn through both loops on the hook in one smooth action. As you use the yarn, allow it to flow through the fingers of your yarn hand while tensioning it gently.

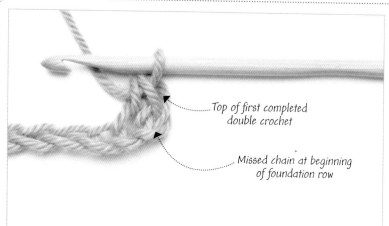

Top of first completed
double crochet

Missed chain at beginning
of foundation row

5 This completes the first double crochet. The missed chain at the beginning of this first row does not count as a stitch on its own (in other words, it is not included when you count how many stitches are in the row and it is not worked into in the next row).

6 Continue across the foundation chain, working one double crochet (dc) into each chain in the same way.

Tip If you want to put down your crochet, remove the hook from the loop and extend the loop to stop it unravelling.

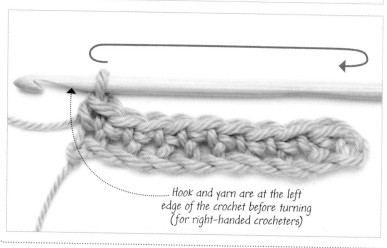

Hook and yarn are at the left
edge of the crochet before turning
(for right-handed crocheters)

7 At the end of the row, turn your crochet to position the yarn and hook at the right edge of the piece of crochet, ready to begin the second row. (For left-handed crocheters, turning will bring the hook and yarn from the right edge to the left edge of the crochet.)

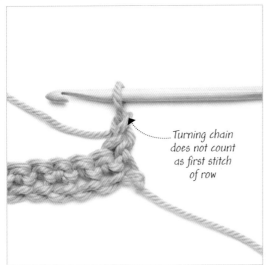

Turning chain
does not count
as first stitch
of row

Insert hook under
both strands
of top of stitch

8 To begin the second row, make one chain stitch. This chain is called the turning chain, and it brings the work up to the height of the double crochet stitches that will follow.

9 Work the first dc into the top of the first stitch in the row below. Always insert the hook under both strands of the "V" of the stitch. Continue across the row.

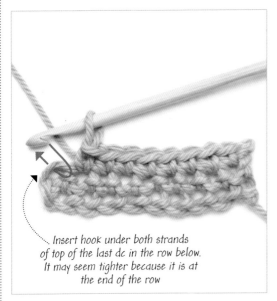

Insert hook under both strands
of top of the last dc in the row below.
It may seem tighter because it is at
the end of the row

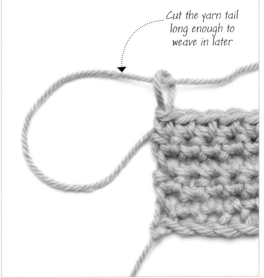

Cut the yarn tail
long enough to
weave in later

10 At the end of the row, work the last stitch into the top of the last dc of the row below. Work following rows as for the second row.

11 When you have completed your crochet, fasten off by cutting the yarn, removing the hook from the loop, and passing the cut yarn through the loop. Pull tight to close.

Counting double crochet stitches

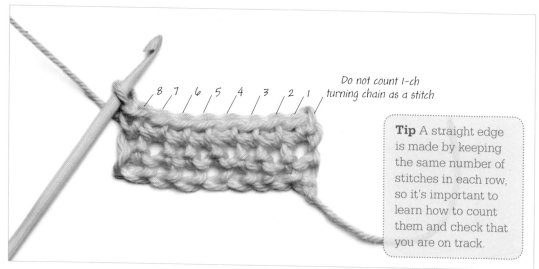

8 7 6 5 4 3 2 1

Do not count 1-ch turning chain as a stitch

Tip A straight edge is made by keeping the same number of stitches in each row, so it's important to learn how to count them and check that you are on track.

With the front of the last row facing you, count the top of each stitch (the "V" shapes). If you are losing stitches as your crochet grows, you may not be working into the last stitch of the row below; if you are gaining stitches, you may have worked twice into the same stitch.

A finished double crochet swatch

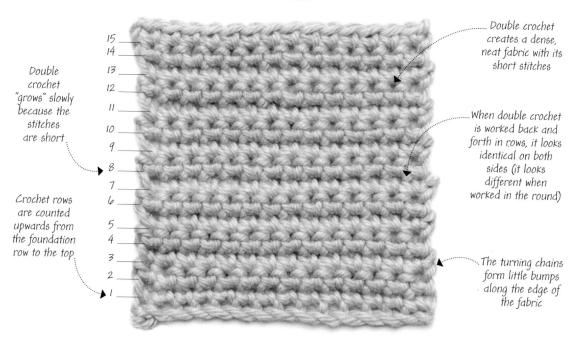

15
14
13
12
11
10
9
8
7
6
5
4
3
2
1

Double crochet "grows" slowly because the stitches are short

Crochet rows are counted upwards from the foundation row to the top

Double crochet creates a dense, neat fabric with its short stitches

When double crochet is worked back and forth in rows, it looks identical on both sides (it looks different when worked in the round)

The turning chains form little bumps along the edge of the fabric

How to **Join in New Yarn and Colours**

Joining in a new ball of yarn and hiding yarn ends are skills you'll use a lot, especially when you're making larger items. For neat results, try to change yarns at the beginning or end of a row.

Joining in new yarn

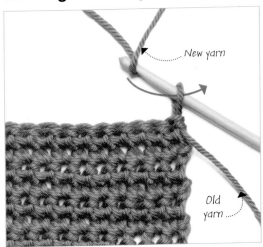

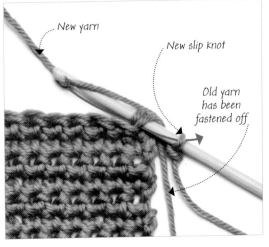

METHOD ONE
Join in a new yarn at the beginning of a row. Drop the old yarn and pull the new yarn through the loop on the hook, then begin the row as usual. Weave in the yarn ends later.

METHOD TWO
Fasten off the old yarn. Using the new yarn, make a slip knot on the hook. Insert the hook in the first stitch of the row and draw a loop through both the stitch and loop on the hook.

Weaving in yarn ends

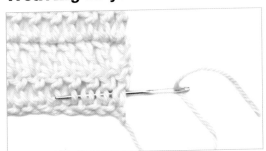

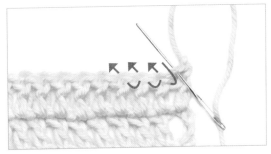

WEAVING IN THROUGH STITCHES
Using a blunt-ended yarn needle, weave the yarn end through the centre of several stitches. Trim off the yarn close to the fabric.

WEAVING IN ALONG TOP OF STITCHES
For a slightly more secure finishing that is good for slippery yarns, you can weave the yarn in and out of the top of the stitches.

Making stripes of colour

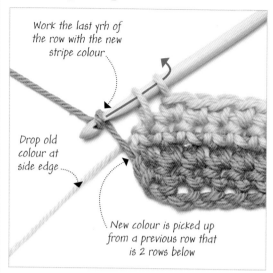

Work the last yrh of the row with the new stripe colour

Drop old colour at side edge

New colour is picked up from a previous row that is 2 rows below

New colour will form first chain of next row

Dropped colour can be picked up again after 2 rows for the next stripe

1 For a smooth transition between colours when working stripes in any stitch, always change to the next colour on the last yrh of the row before the next stripe colour is started.

2 Draw the new colour through the last yrh of the row to complete the previous stitch. The new colour is ready to make the turning chain and start the next stripe.

Carrying colours up side edge

Tip Carrying colours is useful for wide stripes and for 3- or 4-colour stripes.

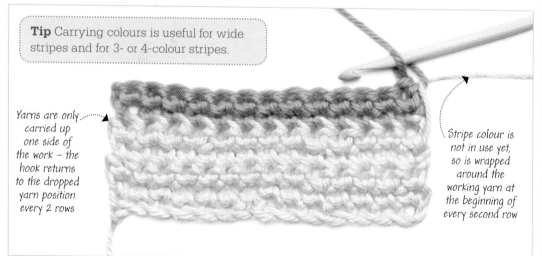

Yarns are only carried up one side of the work – the hook returns to the dropped yarn position every 2 rows

Stripe colour is not in use yet, so is wrapped around the working yarn at the beginning of every second row

If a colour is not needed for more than 2 rows, wrap it around the other colour to secure it until needed. If it is not needed for more than 8 rows, cut it off and join it in again later.

Make a Washcloth

This pretty, practical cotton washcloth can be used in the bath or shower; it is also an effective household cleaning cloth. Worked in rows of double crochet with single-row contrast stripes, it is easy and quick to make.

251 Ecru x 1

356 Blue John x 1

5mm hook

Instructions

Yarn
You can use any DK cotton yarn. Here we have used Rowan Handknit Cotton 50g (85m/95yd) in 2 colours
A: 251 Ecru x 1 ball
B: 356 Blue John x 1 ball

Hook Size
5mm hook

Size
25cm x 23cm (9¾in x 9in)

Pattern
Washcloth
With yarn A, make 37 ch.

Row 1 (RS) 1 dc in 2nd ch from hook, 1 dc in each ch to end, turn. (36sts)

Row 2 1 ch (does not count as st), 1 dc in each dc of previous row, turn.

Rows 3 and 4 Rep row 2; join in yarn B on last dc of row 4, but do not cut yarn A, turn.

Row 5 With RS facing and using yarn B, work 1 ch, 1 dc in each dc to end of row; do not turn but remove hook and pull out loop to prevent it unravelling, then return to beg of row and pick up yarn A.

Row 6 With RS facing and using yarn A, work 1 ch, 1 dc in each dc to end of row, pulling loop of yarn B through last dc; turn.

Row 7 With WS facing and using yarn B, work 1 ch, 1 dc in each dc to end of row; do not turn but remove hook and pull out loop, then return to beg of row and pick up yarn A.

Row 8 With WS facing, using yarn A, work 1 ch, 1 dc in each dc to end of row, pulling loop of yarn B through last dc; turn.

Row 9 With RS facing and using yarn B, work 1 ch, 1 dc in each dc to end of row; cut yarn B and fasten off.

Row 10 With RS facing, return to beg of row, pick up yarn A and work 1 ch, 1 dc in each dc to end of row; turn.

Row 11 1 ch, 1 dc in each dc to end of row.

Rows 12–39 Rep row 11, joining in yarn B on last st of row 39.

Rows 40–45 Rep rows 5–10.

Rows 46–48 Rep row 11.

Row 49 Work 1 ss in each st of previous row; do not fasten off.

Hanging Loop
Work 12 ch and join with ss to 1st of 12 ch. Fasten off, weave in ends.

> **Tip** Numbers in brackets in all patterns, e.g. (12sts), show the number of stitches that should be in the row just completed. This is important for patterns with shaping involved.

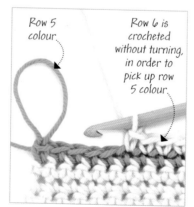

Row 5 colour.

Row 6 is crocheted without turning, in order to pick up row 5 colour.

Pick up new colour
In row 6, the new colour is joined at the beginning of the row just crocheted, rather than at the end of the row. This creates single-row stripes.

Chain loop handle
To make a practical loop handle for your washcloth, make 12 chains at the end of the last row and attach to the first of these chains with a slip stitch.

How to **Work Half Treble Crochet** (Abbreviation = *htr*)

After double crochet, half treble crochet comes next in order of stitch heights (see p.66). It is firm, like double crochet and fairly dense, but produces a slightly softer texture, which makes it ideal for baby garments. It is best to move on to learning how to work half trebles only when you can make double crochet stitches with confidence.

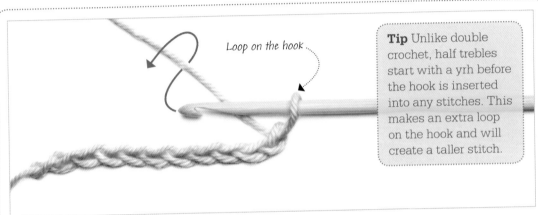

Loop on the hook

Tip Unlike double crochet, half trebles start with a yrh before the hook is inserted into any stitches. This makes an extra loop on the hook and will create a taller stitch.

1 Make a foundation chain as long as you require. To begin the first stitch, wrap the yarn around the hook (yrh) in the usual way, bringing the yarn over the front of the hook.

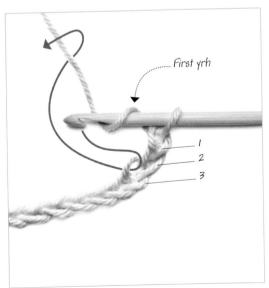

First yrh

1
2
3

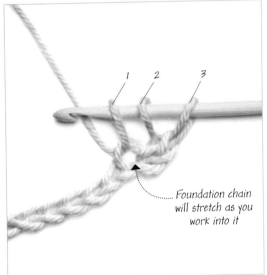

1   2   3

Foundation chain will stretch as you work into it

2 Insert the hook through the third chain from the hook, yrh again (as shown by the large arrow), and draw a loop back through the chain.

3 There are now 3 loops on the hook. (Loop 1 is the yrh just made; loop 2 is the first yrh; loop 3 is the original loop on the hook.)

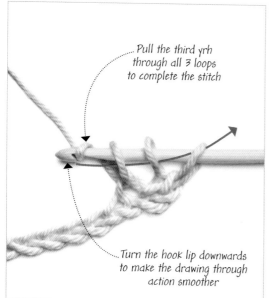

Pull the third yrh through all 3 loops to complete the stitch

Turn the hook lip downwards to make the drawing through action smoother

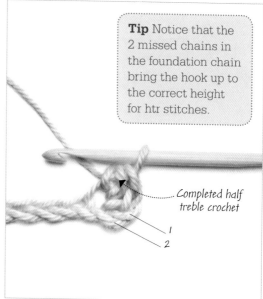

Tip Notice that the 2 missed chains in the foundation chain bring the hook up to the correct height for htr stitches.

Completed half treble crochet

1
2

4 Yrh again and draw a loop through all 3 loops on the hook as shown by the large arrow. (This motion becomes more fluid with practice.)

5 This completes the first half treble crochet stitch (htr). It is roughly twice the height of a double crochet stitch.

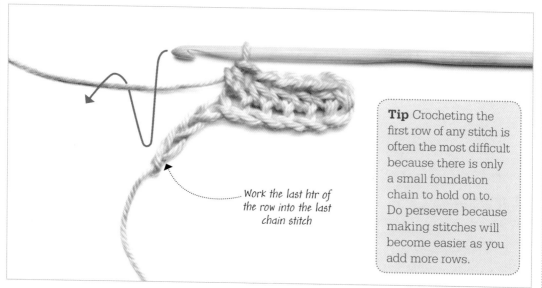

Work the last htr of the row into the last chain stitch

Tip Crocheting the first row of any stitch is often the most difficult because there is only a small foundation chain to hold on to. Do persevere because making stitches will become easier as you add more rows.

6 Continue the first row by working one htr into each chain in the same way. Remember to start each half treble stitch by wrapping the yarn around the hook before inserting it through the chain, keeping an even tension on the yarn (see p.29).

2 chains count as
first stitch of row

7 After working a half treble crochet into the last chain, turn the work to position the yarn at the beginning of the second row. (End of row for right-handers is shown here.)

8 Begin the second row by making 2 chains. These turning chains bring the work up to the height of the half trebles that follow, and also count as the first stitch of the row.

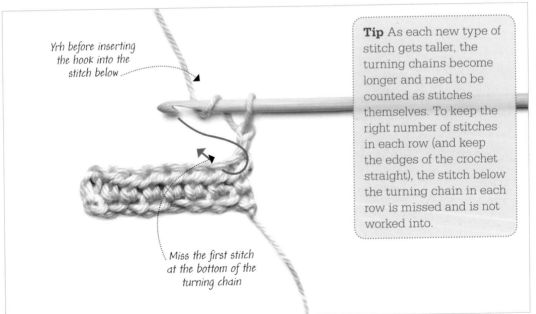

Yrh before inserting the hook into the stitch below

Miss the first stitch at the bottom of the turning chain

Tip As each new type of stitch gets taller, the turning chains become longer and need to be counted as stitches themselves. To keep the right number of stitches in each row (and keep the edges of the crochet straight), the stitch below the turning chain in each row is missed and is not worked into.

9 Yrh and work the first half treble into the top of the second stitch in the row below. Insert the hook under both strands of the "V" to begin the half treble.

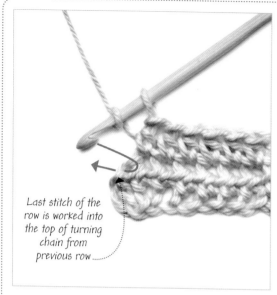

Last stitch of the row is worked into the top of turning chain from previous row

Leave an end at least 10cm (4in) long, so it can be woven in later

10 Work a half treble into each of the remaining half treble stitches in the row below. Work the following rows as for the second row.

11 When the work is complete, cut the yarn. Remove the hook from the loop, pass the yarn end through the loop, and pull tight to close the loop and fasten off securely.

A finished half treble crochet swatch

8

7

6

5

4

3

2

1

Half treble crochet needs fewer rows than double crochet to reach a similiar size. Compare it to the double crochet swatch on page 37

Half treble crochet worked in rows looks the same on both sides, making it a reversible fabric

The short stitches make a close texture, but the extra stitch height gives a softer drape than double crochet

How to **Join with Seams**

You can join pieces of crochet fabric by using either a blunt-ended yarn needle or a crochet hook, and there are various types of seams to try. Backstitch and slip stitch create strong seams with a small ridge on one side, which is ideal for items that will be turned inside out. For flatter seams, try overcast stitch or mattress stitch (see p.48).

Backstitch seam

Yarn first secured with two or three stitches

Forward stitch goes forward two spaces

1 Align the crochet pieces with right sides together and secure the yarn with two or three overcast stitches in the same place. Then, inserting the needle close to the edge, work the seam taking one stitch forwards and one stitch back.

NOTE: Contrasting yarns are used in all of these examples for clarity but usually a matching yarn is used for seams.

Blunt-ended yarn needle

Backward stitch goes back one space, inserted where the previous stitch finished

2 On the backward stitch, be sure to insert the needle through the same place as the end of the last stitch. At the end of the seam, secure the yarn in the same way as at the beginning of the seam.

Tip Backstitch produces durable seams that are excellent for garments and accessories.

Overcast stitch seam (also called whip stitch)

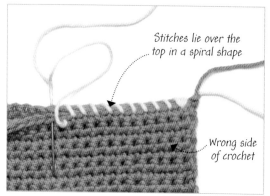

Stitches lie over the top in a spiral shape

Wrong side of crochet

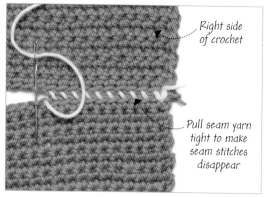

Right side of crochet

Pull seam yarn tight to make seam stitches disappear

SIMPLE OVERCAST SEAM
Align the crochet pieces with right sides together and secure the yarn as for backstitch. Then, inserting the needle close to the edge, make stitches through the two layers as shown above.

FLAT OVERCAST SEAM
For a flat seam along the tops of stitches, place the pieces right-side up and edge-to-edge. Work stitches as for the simple overcast seam, but insert the needle through only the back loops of the stitches.

Slip stitch crocheted seam

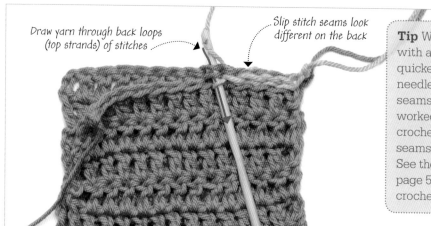

Draw yarn through back loops (top strands) of stitches

Slip stitch seams look different on the back

Tip Working seams with a hook can be quicker than using a needle. Although seams can be worked with double crochet, slip stitch seams are less bulky. See the project on page 50 for a double crochet seam.

1 Align the two layers of crochet with the right sides together. Place a slip knot on a crochet hook, then insert the hook through the two layers at the starting end of the seam. Make a yrh and draw a loop through the two layers and the loop on the hook.

2 Continue in this way, then fasten off at the end. When working the seam along the top edges (as here), insert the hook through only the back loops of the stitches. Along row-end edges, work the hook right through the layers, one stitch in from the edge.

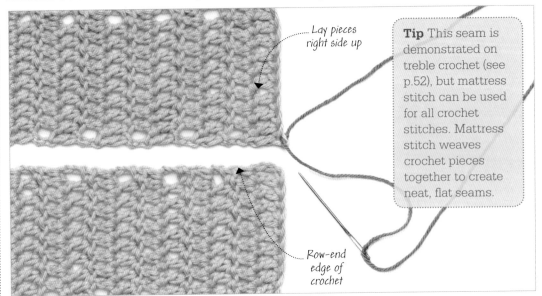

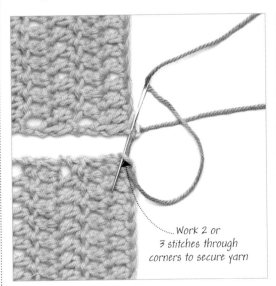

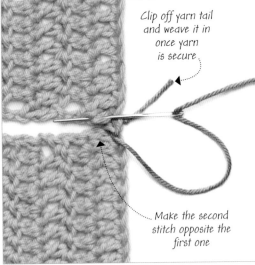

Mattress stitch seam (also called edge-to-edge seam)

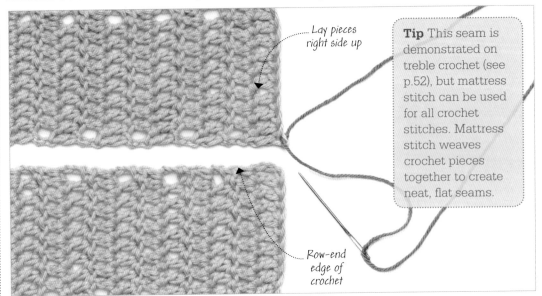

Lay pieces right side up

Tip This seam is demonstrated on treble crochet (see p.52), but mattress stitch can be used for all crochet stitches. Mattress stitch weaves crochet pieces together to create neat, flat seams.

Row-end edge of crochet

1 Lay the crochet pieces right side up and align the row ends edge-to-edge. Insert the needle through the corner of the top piece, leaving a long loose end.

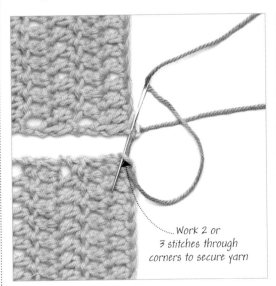

Work 2 or 3 stitches through corners to secure yarn

2 Insert the needle through the corner of the other piece, then through both pieces again in the same place at the corner to secure the yarn firmly.

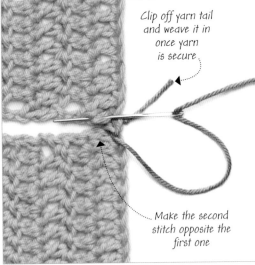

Clip off yarn tail and weave it in once yarn is secure

Make the second stitch opposite the first one

3 Make 2 mattress stitches opposite each other by inserting the needle through the body of the stitches at the edge of the crochet, first on one piece of crochet then on the other.

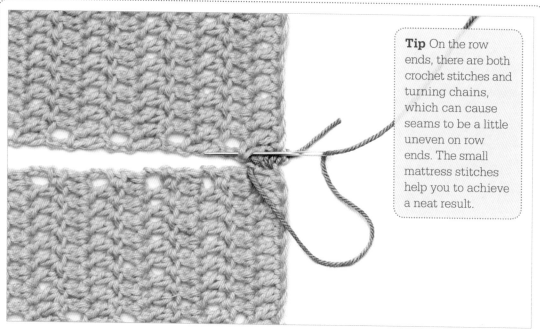

Tip On the row ends, there are both crochet stitches and turning chains, which can cause seams to be a little uneven on row ends. The small mattress stitches help you to achieve a neat result.

4 Make the next pair of stitches in the same way, working the needle through a stitch or turning chain on one piece of crochet, then again on the opposite piece.

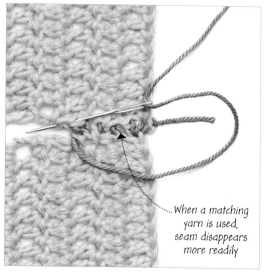

When a matching yarn is used, seam disappears more readily

5 Continue along the seam, taking a stitch in each side alternately. Take shorter stitches on each piece if the yarn used (for the crochet pieces) is bulky.

6 After every few stitches, pull the seam yarn tight so that it almost disappears on the right side of the crochet. At the end of the seam, secure the yarn and darn in the ends.

Make a Phone Cover

Everyone carries a phone these days and a cover will not only help you to identify yours, but it will also protect the screen from scratches and bumps. In addition, it's a great way to practise half treble stitches. Choose from a case with a flap or a simpler one with a button loop closure.

Instructions

Yarn

You can use any Aran weight cotton or cotton blend yarn, making sure that it works to the correct tension for this pattern. Here we have used Rowan Summer Tweed 50g (120m/131yd) in 2 colours
A: 00544 Jardinier x 1 ball
B: 00547 Navy x 1 ball

00544 Jardinier x 1   **00547 Navy x 1**

4mm hook

Hook Size

4mm hook

Notions

Design 1: 24mm (1in) buttons x 2
Design 2: 30mm (1½in) button x 1
Sewing thread to match buttons

Tension

16 htr and 12 rows to 10cm (4in)

Size

13.5cm x 8cm (5½in x 3¼in)

Pattern

Phone cover with flap

With yarn A, make 13 ch.
Row 1 (RS) 1 htr in 3rd ch from hook, 1 htr in each ch to end. (12 sts)
Row 2 2 ch (counts as 1 htr), 1 htr in each of next 10 htr, 1 htr in top of 2-ch.
Rep row 2 34 times.
Row 36 1 ch (does not count as a st), 1 dc in first htr, 2 ch (to form buttonhole, see tip), miss 2 htr, 1 dc in each of next 6 htr, 2 ch, miss 2 htr, 1 dc in top of 2-ch.
Row 37 1 ch, 1 dc in first dc, 2 dc in 2-ch sp, 1 dc in each of next 6 dc, 2 dc in 2-ch sp, 1 dc in last dc.
Cut yarn and fasten off.

Making up and border

Fold along top of row 14. Beg at bottom, at edge of fold, with RS facing and buttonhole edge towards the left, join in yarn B and work 1 ch (does not count as a st), then work 18 dc along side edges, inserting the hook through both thicknesses to create a decorative seam; when you reach the top edge of the front of the case, continue working along edge through single thickness up side of flap, working 8 dc, evenly spaced, then 3 dc in corner, 1 dc in each htr across top edge, 3 dc in corner, 8 dc down opposite side of flap, then through double thickness, 18 dc, evenly spaced, along side edges down to bottom corner. Cut yarn and fasten off.
Stitch buttons to front of case, to correspond with buttonholes.

Phone cover with button loop

With yarn A, make 13 ch.
Row 1 (RS) 1 htr in 3rd ch from hook, 1 htr in each ch to end. (12 sts)
Row 2 2 ch (counts as 1 htr), 1 htr in each of next 10 htr, 1 htr in top of 2-ch.
Rep row 2 26 times.
Cut yarn and fasten off.

Making up and border

Fold in half and join sides with a double crochet seam with yarn A.
Cut yarn and fasten off.
Border Row 1: Beg at top of one of the side seams, join in yarn B and work 1 ch (does not count as a st), 1 dc in each of next 12 htr along top edge, 1 dc in side seam, continue along top edge on other side and work 1 dc in each htr, 1 dc in side seam, join with ss to 1st dc. (26 sts)
Border Row 2: 1 ch, 1 dc in each of next 13 sts along one edge, continue along top edge on other side and work 1 dc in each of next 5 sts, 18 ch to create button loop, miss next 2 sts, 1 dc in each of next 6 sts to end of row, join with a ss to 1st dc.
Cut yarn and fasten off; weave in all ends.
Stitch button to front of case, to correspond with button loop.

> **Tip** A button loop is very easy to make: chain stitches worked on an edge form a loop. A buttonhole is made with a combination of chain stitches and missed stitches within the body or edge of a crocheted piece (see p.58 for more about this technique).

How to **Work Treble Crochet** (Abbreviation = tr)

Versatile treble crochet is the most frequently used crochet stitch. As
a tall stitch, it produces a softer and more open crochet fabric and it
grows quickly too – it's easy to see why it's such a popular stitch. It
can also be combined to create lots of textures and decorative stitches,
which will be explored in parts two and three of the course.

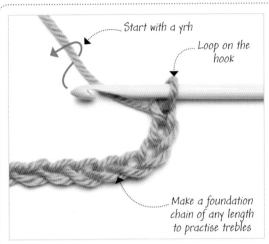

Start with a yrh

Loop on the hook

Make a foundation chain of any length to practise trebles

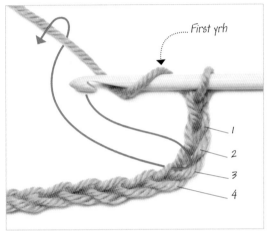

First yrh

1
2
3
4

1 Make a foundation chain as long as you require. To begin the first stitch, wrap the yarn around the hook (yrh).

2 Insert the hook through the fourth chain from the hook, yrh again (as shown by the large arrow), and draw a loop back through the chain.

1   2   3

Draw the hook through the first 2 loops only

3 There are now 3 loops on the hook. (Loop 1 is the yrh just made; loop 2 is the first yrh; loop 3 is the original loop on the hook.)

4 Yrh and draw a loop through the first 2 loops on the hook. Be careful not to draw through all the loops (like a half treble crochet).

Yrh again and draw through the remaining loops to complete the stitch

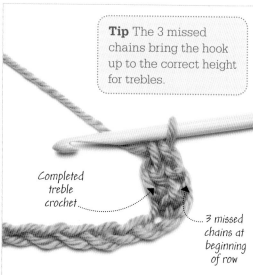

Tip The 3 missed chains bring the hook up to the correct height for trebles.

Completed treble crochet

3 missed chains at beginning of row

5 There are now 2 loops left on the hook. Yrh a fourth and final time and draw a loop through the remaining 2 loops. This completes the first treble (tr).

6 The finished treble is about three times taller than a double crochet. The 3 missed chains at the beginning of the chain count as the first treble stitch of the foundation row.

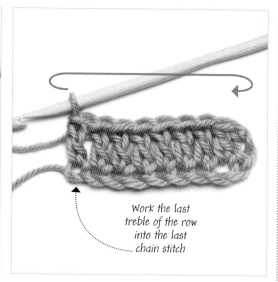

Work the last treble of the row into the last chain stitch

7 Continue along the row, working one tr into each chain stitch in the same way. Remember to start each stitch with a yrh before inserting the hook through the chain.

8 After the last treble crochet stitch of the foundation row has been completed, turn the work to position the yarn at the beginning of the second row.

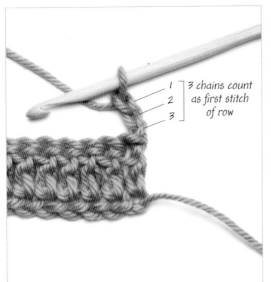

1 ⎤
2 ⎥ 3 chains count
3 ⎦ as first stitch of row

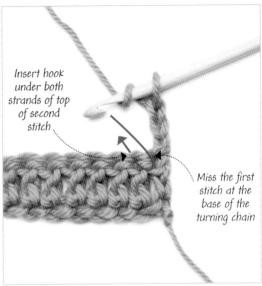

Insert hook under both strands of top of second stitch

Miss the first stitch at the base of the turning chain

9 To begin the second row of treble crochet, make 3 chain stitches. This brings the work up to the correct height.

10 Yrh, then, missing the first treble in the row below, work the first tr into the top of the second stitch.

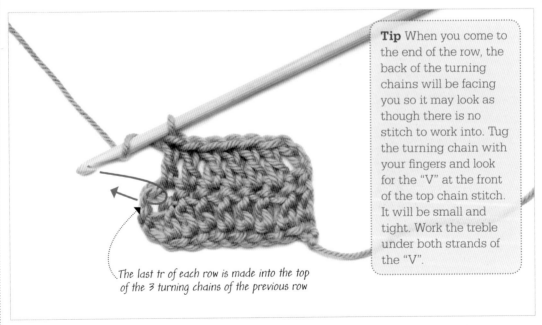

The last tr of each row is made into the top of the 3 turning chains of the previous row

Tip When you come to the end of the row, the back of the turning chains will be facing you so it may look as though there is no stitch to work into. Tug the turning chain with your fingers and look for the "V" at the front of the top chain stitch. It will be small and tight. Work the treble under both strands of the "V".

11 Continue along the second row, working a tr into each stitch, making the last stitch into the top of the 3 chains of the row below. Work following rows in the same way.

Counting treble crochet

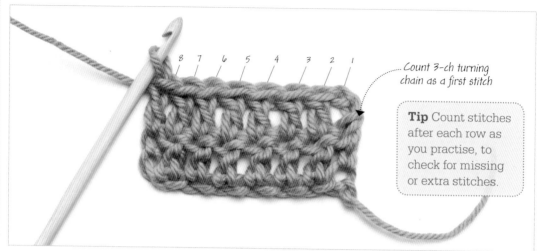

8 7 6 5 4 3 2 1

Count 3-ch turning chain as a first stitch

Tip Count stitches after each row as you practise, to check for missing or extra stitches.

With the front of the last row facing you, count the turning chain as the first stitch, then count the top of each treble. If you are losing stitches as your crochet grows, you are probably not working into the top of the turning chain; if you are gaining stitches, you may be working into the first treble of the row, instead of missing it.

A finished treble crochet swatch

6
5
4
3
2
1

The fabric is soft and airy because of the taller stitch height

Treble crochet works up quickly, needing fewer rows to make a square

There are natural gaps at the edges of rows where there is a turning chain

Treble crochet worked in rows is a reversible fabric, just like all the other basic stitches

55

Make a Cafetière Cosy

Never suffer cold coffee again – this elegant treble crochet cosy is designed to wrap twice around a cafetière to keep your coffee warm. It is cleverly made by crocheting the fastening strap directly onto the cosy.

Instructions

Yarn

You can use any DK wool or wool blend yarn. Here we have used Rowan Wool Cotton DK 50g (113m/123yd) in 2 colours
A: 00903 Misty x 1 ball
B: 00941 Clear x 1 ball

Hook Size

4mm hook

Notions

28mm (1⅛in) button x 1
Sewing thread to match button

Tension

17 tr and 10 rows to 10cm (4in)

Size

To fit a standard 8-cup cafetière
Dimensions: 17cm (6¾in) tall x 31cm (12¼in) circumference
Handle width 10cm (4in)

Special Note

Foundation chain should fit cafetière height; adjust if needed.

Pattern
Cafetière Cosy

With yarn A, make 31 ch (foundation ch should be worked loosely: use a larger hook, if necessary, to ensure chains are loose).

Row 1 (RS) 1 dc in 2nd ch from hook, 1 dc in each ch to end of row, turn. (30 sts)

Row 2 3 ch (counts as 1 tr), 1 tr in next dc, 1 tr in each dc to end of row, turn.

Row 3 3 ch, 1 tr in next tr, 1 tr in each tr to end of row, working last tr in top of 3-ch, turn.
Rep row 3 27 times until piece measures 28.5cm (11¼in), or desired length. Cut yarn and fasten off; turn.

00903 Misty x 1

00941 Clear x 1

4mm hook

Strap

With RS of work facing and last row uppermost, miss first 6 tr and join yarn B to next tr.

Row 1 3 ch, 1 tr in next tr, 1 tr in each of next 16 tr; turn. (18 sts)
Rep row 1 38 times until piece measures 40cm (15¾in), or the desired length.

Next row 1 ch (does not count as a st), 1 dc in each of first 7 tr, 4 ch (to form buttonhole), miss 4 tr, 1 dc in each of next 7 tr.

Next row 1 ch, 1 dc in each of first 7 dc, 4 dc in 4-ch sp, 1 dc in each dc to end of row.
Fasten off and weave in all ends.

Join the contrast yarn to the 7th treble stitch

Beginning the strap

The strap of the cafetière is made by joining yarn B to the 7th treble stitch along the row, with the right side of the work facing you. Then work 3 chains (counts as the first treble stitch) and continue working in treble stitch.

Finishing

Press work lightly under a damp cloth to neaten edges. Wrap the cosy and its strap around the cafetière and mark the position of the button with a pin. Remove the cosy, stitch on the button, and place the finished cosy onto the cafetière.

Tip Although you can use any wool or wool blend yarn for this project, the equal blend of merino wool and cotton that we have used here has two main advantages: the wool element provides good insulation, and the cotton gives good stitch definition, so the beauty of the treble stitch is accentuated.

Making buttonholes

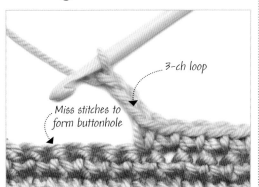

3-ch loop

Miss stitches to form buttonhole

1 To make buttonholes along an edge, work in double crochet to the position of the buttonhole. Make 2, 3, or more chains, depending on the size of the button. Miss the same number of stitches and work the next double crochet in the next stitch.

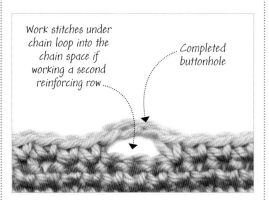

Work stitches under chain loop into the chain space if working a second reinforcing row

Completed buttonhole

2 Continue working double crochet and buttonholes until the edging is complete. To make stronger buttonholes, work a second row of double crochet on top of the first row, working stitches under the chain loop when you reach it.

Work last treble of each row into top of 3-chain of previous row to keep a straight edge

This edge wraps around the cafetière, either side of the handle. If needed, adjust number of rows to fit your own cafetière

This edge fits the height of the cafetière. Alter the number of foundation chains if you need to adjust the fit

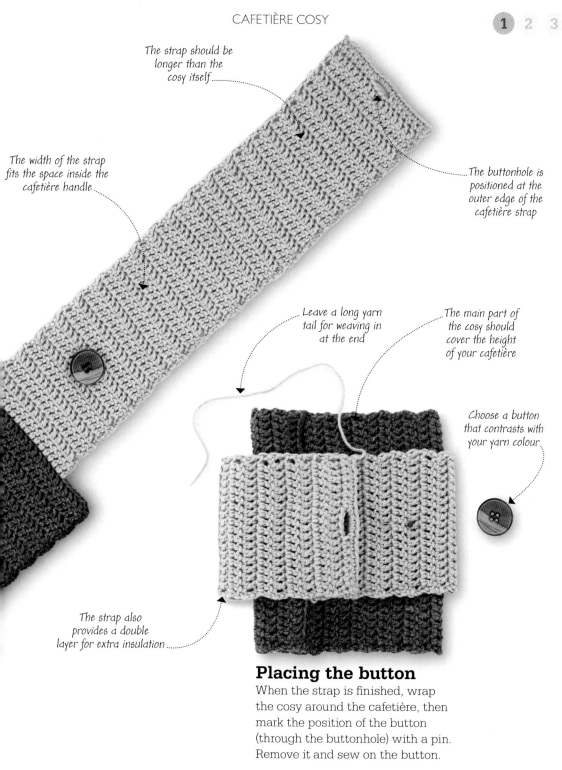

The strap should be longer than the cosy itself

The width of the strap fits the space inside the cafetière handle

The buttonhole is positioned at the outer edge of the cafetière strap

Leave a long yarn tail for weaving in at the end

The main part of the cosy should cover the height of your cafetière

Choose a button that contrasts with your yarn colour

The strap also provides a double layer for extra insulation

Placing the button

When the strap is finished, wrap the cosy around the cafetière, then mark the position of the button (through the buttonhole) with a pin. Remove it and sew on the button.

How to **Work Double Treble Crochet** (Abbreviation = *dtr*)

Worked similarly to treble crochet, double treble crochet stitches are one chain length taller because the stitch is begun with two wraps instead of only one (see p.52). Double treble crochet is often used in lacy patterns and in crochet blocks (see p.161–165) because their height helps to add shape.

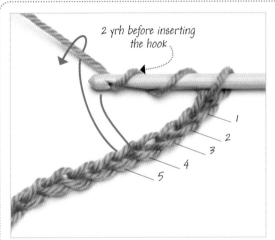

1 Make a foundation chain as long as you require. Wrap the yarn twice around the hook (yrh) and then insert the hook through the fifth chain from the hook.

2 Yrh and draw a loop through the chain. There are now 4 loops on the hook. Yrh again and draw a loop through the first 2 loops on the hook.

3 There are now 3 loops remaining. Yrh and draw a loop through the first 2 loops on the hook.

4 There are 2 loops remaining. Yrh and draw a loop through both these loops. This completes the first double treble (dtr).

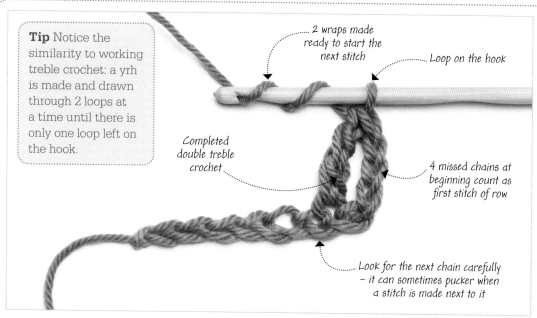

Tip Notice the similarity to working treble crochet: a yrh is made and drawn through 2 loops at a time until there is only one loop left on the hook.

2 wraps made ready to start the next stitch

Loop on the hook

Completed double treble crochet

4 missed chains at beginning count as first stitch of row

Look for the next chain carefully – it can sometimes pucker when a stitch is made next to it

5 As for all tall crochet stitches, the missed chain stitches at the beginning of the foundation chain count as the first stitch of the foundation row. Work one dtr into each chain in the same way, making sure to yrh twice before making each stitch.

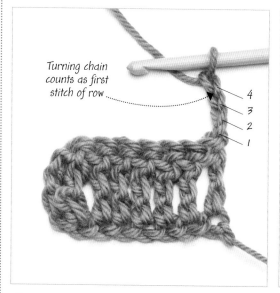

Turning chain counts as first stitch of row

4
3
2
1

Miss the first stitch below the turning chain

6 At the end of the foundation row, turn the crochet and begin the second row with a 4-chain turning chain.

7 Miss the top of the first double treble in the row below and work the first dtr into the top of the second stitch.

Tip The missed stitches blend in easily with the airy look of finished double treble crochet.

Work into the top stitch of the 4 chains in the row below to complete second row

First double treble at beginning of second row is not worked into

8 Work a dtr into each of the remaining double trebles in the row below. Work the last stitch of the row into the top of the 4 chains – the back of the chain will be facing you, so look carefully for the front "V". Work following rows as for the second row.

A finished double treble crochet swatch

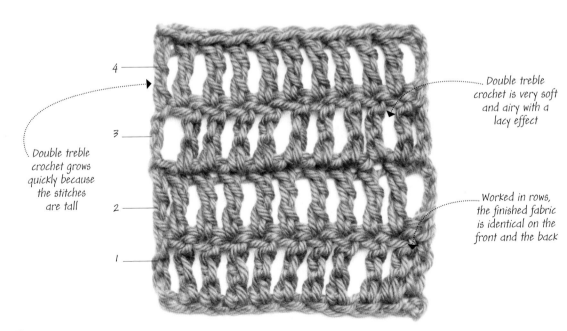

Double treble crochet is very soft and airy with a lacy effect

Double treble crochet grows quickly because the stitches are tall

Worked in rows, the finished fabric is identical on the front and the back

4

3

2

1

How to **Work Triple Treble Crochet** (Abbreviation = *trtr*)

All taller stitches are worked in the same way as double trebles, except that more wraps are wound around the hook before the stitch is begun and they require taller turning chains. Once you can work triple trebles easily, you will be able to work quadruple and quintuple trebles without much effort. You'll find taller stitches used in decorative patterns such as flowers and snowflakes.

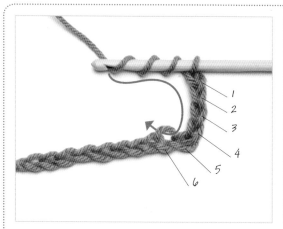

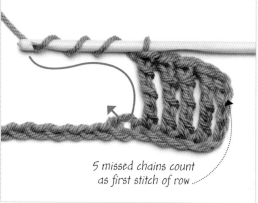

5 missed chains count as first stitch of row

1 Wrap the yarn 3 times around the hook and insert the hook through the sixth stitch from the hook. Yrh and work the loops off the hook two at a time, as for double trebles.

2 Continue along the row, wrapping the yarn 3 times around the hook before starting each stitch. Start the second and following rows with 5 chains.

A finished triple treble crochet swatch

3

2

1

The taller the stitch, the more quickly it works up.

Triple treble crochet worked in rows looks the same on both sides of the fabric

Notice how airy the crochet texture becomes as you move from double crochet to the taller stitches

Make a Towel Edging

Trim a towel with a simple edging, to bring a bit of
glamour to the bathroom. This edging helps you to
practise a range of basic stitches, uses very little yarn,
and is surprisingly quick to do.

Instructions

Yarn

You can use any 4-ply mercerized cotton yarn. Here we have used Rowan Siena 4-ply 50g (140m/153yd) 668 Beacon x 1 ball

Hook Size

3mm hook

Notions

Sewing thread to match yarn colour

Tension

18 sts to 10cm (4in)

Size

One pattern repeat (9sts) measures 5cm (2in), so it is easy to calculate how many foundation chains to work to make an edging to fit your towel (work 9 foundation ch per pattern repeat, plus 1 ch extra). The instructions given here fit a towel 40cm (15¾in) wide.

Pattern

Make 73 ch.
Row 1 (RS) 1 dc in 2nd ch from

668 Beacon x 1

3mm hook

hook, 1 dc in each ch to end, turn. (72sts)
Row 2 1 ch (does not count as a st), 1 dc in each dc to end, turn.
Row 3 1 ch, 1 dc in first st, *1 htr in next st, 1 tr in next st, 1 dtr in next st, 1trtr in next st, 1 dtr in next st, 1 tr in next st, 1 htr in next st, 1 dc in each of next 2 sts; rep from * 7 times, 1 htr in next st, 1 tr in next st, 1 dtr in next st, 1 trtr in next st, 1 dtr in next st, 1 tr in next st, 1 htr in next st, 1 dc in last st, turn.
Row 4 1 ch, 1 dc in each of first 5 sts, *3 ch, 1 dc in same st (trtr of previous row) as last dc, 1 dc in

each of next 9 sts, rep from * to last 4 sts, 1 dc in each of last 4 sts. Fasten off, weave in ends.

Finishing

Press work lightly under a damp cloth. After pressing the edging, pin it in place on the towel, with the row of double crochet overlapping the edge of the towel. Thread a sewing needle with cotton thread to match the edging and, using slip stitch (see below left), sew foundation chain to towel, using small neat stitches.

Stitching in place

Make pairs of small parallel stitches (called slip stitches in sewing), first on the edging then on the towel, to create an almost invisible join.

Calculating length

Make and measure one pattern repeat to calculate how many pattern repeats, and therefore foundations chains, you need for your towel.

How to **Identify Stitches**

As you practise the basic crochet stitches, you will become more familiar
with their structures and it will be much easier to spot and correct mistakes.
Learning to read crochet symbols will help in this process, as they show you
visually how a pattern works. Included here is an introduction to reading basic
stitches in symbols, but there is a more detailed explanation on page 124.

Stitch heights

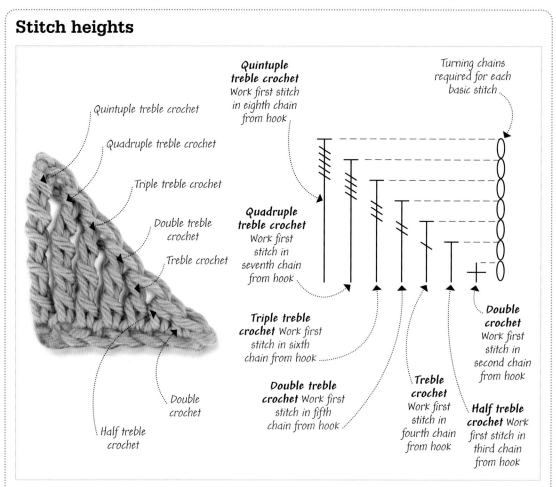

Quintuple treble crochet

Quadruple treble crochet

Triple treble crochet

Double treble crochet

Treble crochet

Double crochet

Half treble crochet

Quintuple treble crochet Work first stitch in eighth chain from hook

Quadruple treble crochet Work first stitch in seventh chain from hook

Turning chains required for each basic stitch

Triple treble crochet Work first stitch in sixth chain from hook

Double treble crochet Work first stitch in fifth chain from hook

Treble crochet Work first stitch in fourth chain from hook

Double crochet Work first stitch in second chain from hook

Half treble crochet Work first stitch in third chain from hook

The photograph above shows each of the
basic stitches in height order; the diagram
shows the same stitches in symbols. The
diagram is a useful reference because it
illustrates approximately how tall each stitch
is in terms of chain stitches – double crochet
is roughly one chain tall, a half treble crochet
is two chains tall, and so on. These heights
determine the number of turning chains you
need to make at the beginning of each row for
each of the basic stitches. The diagram also
shows which chain in the foundation chain
to work into when making the first stitch of
the first row.

Double crochet instructions

Tip Crochet symbols roughly imitate the size and shape of the stitch, and the diagram's rows are read back and forth in the same way that rows are crocheted back and forth. Left-handed crocheters will need to work the diagram in reverse.

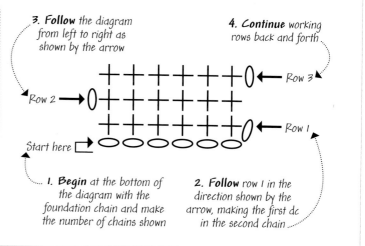

3. Follow the diagram from left to right as shown by the arrow

4. Continue working rows back and forth

Row 2

Row 3

Row 1

Start here

1. Begin at the bottom of the diagram with the foundation chain and make the number of chains shown

2. Follow row 1 in the direction shown by the arrow, making the first dc in the second chain

DOUBLE CROCHET IN ABBREVIATIONS
Make 7 ch.
Row 1 1 dc in 2nd ch from hook, 1 dc in each of rem ch to end, turn.

Row 2 1 ch (does not count as a st), 1 dc in each dc to end, turn.
Rep row 2 to form dc fabric.

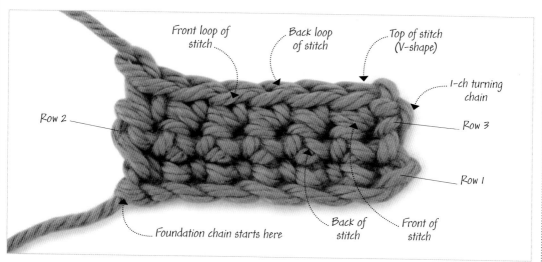

Front loop of stitch

Back loop of stitch

Top of stitch (V-shape)

1-ch turning chain

Row 2

Row 3

Row 1

Foundation chain starts here

Back of stitch

Front of stitch

DOUBLE CROCHET IN FOCUS
Follow the stitch diagram above to make three rows of double crochet. Look at your sample and see if you can identify all the parts of the stitches labelled above. Once you are familiar with the structure of double crochet, you can try simple variations by working into different parts of the stitch, such as front and back loops (see pp.69–71).

Treble crochet instructions

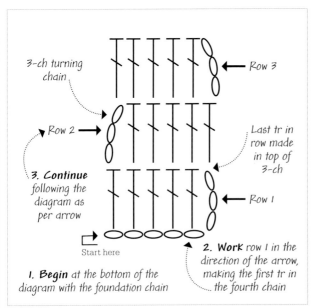

3-ch turning chain

Row 3

Row 2 →

Last tr in row made in top of 3-ch

3. Continue following the diagram as per arrow

Row 1

Start here

2. Work row 1 in the direction of the arrow, making the first tr in the fourth chain

1. Begin at the bottom of the diagram with the foundation chain

TREBLE CROCHET IN ABBREVIATIONS
Make 8 ch.
Row 1 (RS) 1 tr in 4th ch from hook, 1 tr in each of rem ch to end, turn.
Row 2 3 ch (counts as first tr), miss first tr in row below, *1 tr in next tr; rep from * to end, then work 1 tr in top of 3-ch at end, turn.
Rep row 2 to form tr fabric.

Tip The treble symbol has a short diagonal line across its "waist". The diagram shows clearly how the 3-chain turning chain counts as the first stitch of each row.

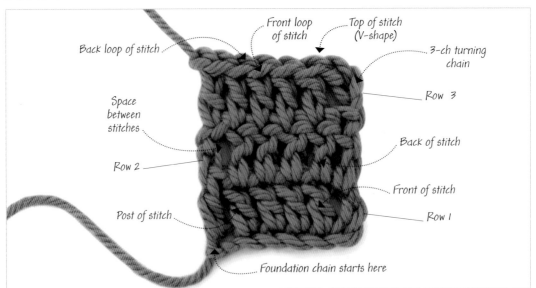

Back loop of stitch

Front loop of stitch

Top of stitch (V-shape)

3-ch turning chain

Row 3

Space between stitches

Back of stitch

Row 2

Front of stitch

Post of stitch

Row 1

Foundation chain starts here

TREBLE CROCHET IN FOCUS
Follow the stitch diagram above to make three rows of treble crochet. See if you can identify all the parts of the stitches labelled above. As a taller stitch, the body of treble crochet forms a "post" with space around it. You can try variations by working into different parts of the stitch, including back loops and between stitches (see p.70).

How to **Work Simple Variations and Textures**

You can work some attractive variations on the basic stitches by working into different parts of the stitch, instead of under the two strands of the V-shape at the top. Working stitches under just one strand, or loop, will create a ridged effect. Taller stitches, such as trebles, have more space around them, which also allows you to work between the stitches.

Working into the back loop of a double crochet

Working into only the back loops of the stitches in every row of double crochet creates a deep ridged effect. The ridges are formed by the unworked loops.

Working into front loop of a double crochet

Front loops are the ones facing you

Working into only the front loops of stitches in every row of double crochet creates a less pronounced ridged texture than working into only the back loops.

Working into the back loop of a treble crochet

The same techniques of working into the front or back loop of a stitch can be used for all crochet stitches to create ridges. The fabric looks the same on both sides. Back loop treble crochet creates wide ridges.

Working into spaces between stitches

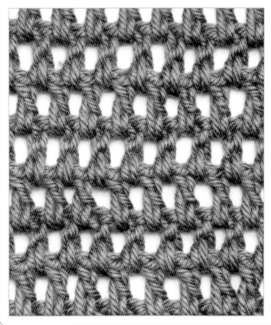

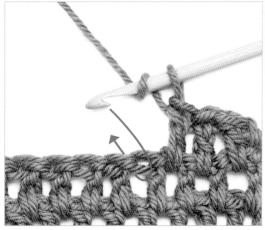

Another way to achieve a subtly different texture with tall basic stitches is to work the stitches into the spaces between the stitches in the row below, instead of into the tops of the stitches.

How to **Work into Chain Spaces**

In many stitch patterns, chain stitches are introduced between the main stitches to create holes or spaces in the fabric. Working into these chain spaces creates an even wider range of pattern effects.

Recognizing chain spaces

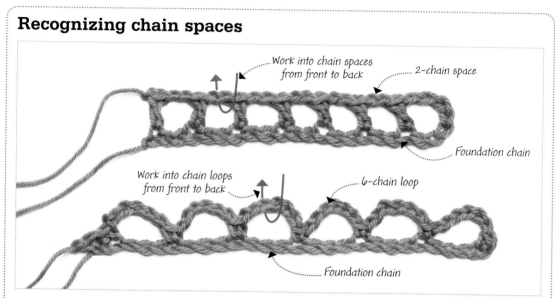

Work into chain spaces from front to back

2-chain space

Foundation chain

Work into chain loops from front to back

6-chain loop

Foundation chain

Spaces formed by short chains are called chain spaces; those formed by long chains are called chain loops. When a crochet pattern instructs you to work into a chain space or loop, always insert your hook through the space and not into the actual chain stitches.

Tweed stitch

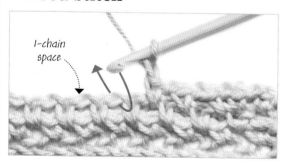

1-chain space

Tweed stitch illustrates the simplest of all textures created by working into a chain space. The double crochet stitches are worked in the 1-chain spaces between the stitches in the row below, instead of into the tops of the stitches.

TWEED STITCH PATTERN
This is a very popular stitch and is a perfect alternative to basic double crochet. (See pp.22–23 for abbreviations.) Start with an even number of chains.
Row 1 1 dc in 2nd ch from hook, *1 ch, miss next ch, 1 dc in next ch; rep from * to end, turn.
Row 2 1 ch (does not count as a stitch), 1 dc in first dc, 1 dc in next 1-ch sp, *1 ch, 1 dc in next 1-ch sp; rep from * to last dc, 1 dc in last dc, turn.
Row 3 1 ch (does not count as a stitch), 1 dc in first dc, *1 ch, 1 dc in next 1-ch sp; rep from * to last 2 dc, 1 ch, miss next dc, 1 dc in last dc, turn.
Rep rows 2 and 3 to form patt.

Make Friendship Bracelets

These bracelets are a great way to practise working into front loops, back loops, and creating chain loops using the fundamental crochet stitches: chain and slip stitch. Make an armful of bracelets for yourself, or to give away as presents, raiding your button box for suitable fastenings.

Instructions

Yarn

You can use any 4-ply cotton or cotton blend yarn. Here we have used Bergère de France Coton Fifty 50g (140m/153yd) in 6 colours
A: 239-56 Petrolier x 1 ball
B: 244-20 Turquoise x 1 ball
C: 293-11 Clementine x 1 ball
D: 219-76 Perle x 1 ball
E: 246-60 Bengale x 1 ball
F: 253-07 Herbage x 1 ball

Hook Size

2mm hook

Notions

A small button for each bracelet

Size

Patterns adapt to fit wearer

Pattern

Multi-chain Bracelet

With yarn A, *make 86 ch (or any number of chains to fit wrist), ss into 1st ch, rep from * once more, then work 8 ch, ss into first of 8-ch to form button loop.
Cut yarn and fasten off. Fold both chains in half and join looped ends. Weave in yarn ends and stitch button in place where loops join.

A: 239-56 Petrolier x 1

B: 244-20 Turquoise x 1

C: 293-11 Clementine x 1

D: 219-76 Perle x 1

E: 246-60 Bengale x 1

F: 253-07 Herbage x 1

2mm hook

Small Scallop Bracelet

With yarn B, make 43 ch (or an odd number of chains to fit wrist).
Row 1 *1 ch, ss in next st, rep from * to last st, 1 ch, ss in last ch; turn and work along opposite side of foundation ch.
Row 2 As row 1; do not cut yarn but work 8 ch, ss into first of 8-ch to form button loop.
Cut yarn and fasten off.
Weave in yarn ends and stitch button in place on opposite end to button loop.

Medium Scallop Bracelet

With yarn C, make 43 ch (or an odd number of chains to fit wrist).
Row 1 *2 ch, ss in next st, rep from * to last st, 2 ch, ss in last ch; turn and work along opposite side of foundation chain.
Row 2 As row 1; do not cut yarn but work 8 ch, ss into first of 8-ch to form button loop.
Cut yarn and fasten off.
Weave in yarn ends and stitch button in place on opposite end to button loop.

Large Scallop Bracelet

With yarn D, make 43 ch (or an odd number of chains to fit wrist).
Row 1 *3 ch, ss in next st, rep from * to last st, 3 ch, ss in last ch; turn and work along opposite side of foundation chain.
Row 2 As row 1; do not cut yarn but work 8 ch, ss into first of 8-ch to form button loop.
Cut yarn and fasten off.
Weave in yarn ends and stitch button in place on opposite end to button loop.

Flat Cord Bracelet

With yarn E, make 43 ch (or an odd number of chains to fit wrist).

Row 1 ss in 2nd ch from hook, ss in each ch to end, turn. (42sts)

Row 2 1 ch, ss into each ss of previous row, inserting hook into back loop only of every st; do not turn, work 8 ch, ss into first of 8-ch to form button loop.

Cut yarn and fasten off.

Weave in yarn ends and stitch button in place on opposite end to button loop.

Square Cord Bracelet

With yarn F, make 43 ch (or an odd number of chains to fit wrist).

Row 1 Ss in 2nd ch from hook, ss in each ch to end, turn. (42sts)

Row 2 1 ch, ss into each ss of previous row, inserting hook into front loop only of every st; turn.

Row 3 As row 2; do not turn, but work 8 ch, ss into first of 8-ch to form button loop.

Cut yarn and fasten off.

Weave in yarn ends and stitch button in place on opposite end to button loop.

Multi-chain Bracelet
Chains

Small Scallop Bracelet
1-ch picot

Medium Scallop Bracelet
2-ch picot

Large Scallop Bracelet
3-ch picot

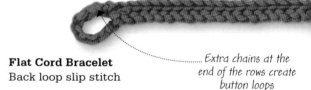

Flat Cord Bracelet
Back loop slip stitch

Extra chains at the end of the rows create button loops

Back loop

Front loop

Back loop slip stitch

Working slip stitches into back loops creates a flat, even fabric. The tops of slip stitches tilt to one side, so the back loop will be the top strand.

Square Cord Bracelet
Front loop slip stitch

Two long chain lengths are doubled up and joined to create four strands

Small chain loops called picots form the scallops

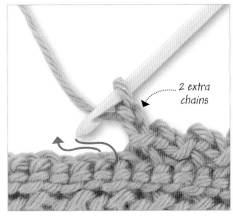

2 extra chains

Working picots

The ruffled edges on the scallop bracelets are created by picots, or tiny chain loops. Extra chains are made before working into the next stitch in the row (shown above).

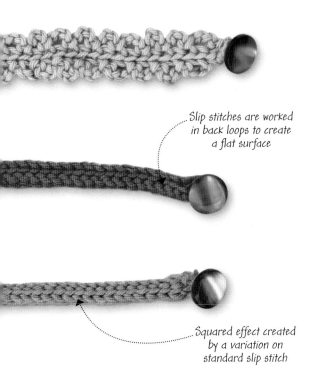

Slip stitches are worked in back loops to create a flat surface

Squared effect created by a variation on standard slip stitch

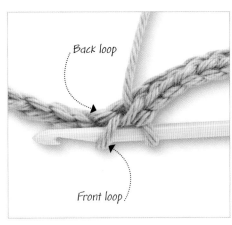

Back loop

Front loop

Front loop slip stitch

Working slip stitches into front loops produces a squared surface. Look carefully for the front loops in the row below as the surface of the crochet will twist to create the squared effect.

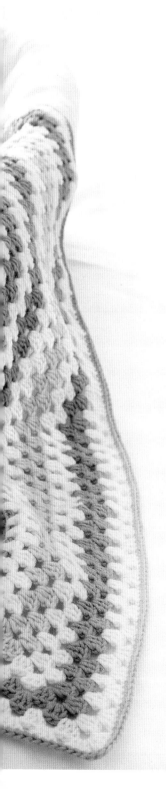

2

Build On It

Now that you can crochet all the basic stitches in rows, it is time to learn to work in the round and discover how to shape your crochet fabric. Working in the round allows you to make some of the most popular crochet items: hats, toys, and the iconic granny square pattern. You will also learn how to combine stitches to create textures, enabling you to make some gorgeous stitch patterns. Practise the new techniques with a variety of satisfying projects, such as a cute baby's hat, a granny square blanket, a pretty clutch bag, and others.

Learn to crochet:

Set of Coasters
pp.80–81

Baby's Hat
pp.106–109

Project Basket
pp.114–115

Bookmark
pp.120–121

How to **Crochet Flat Circles**

Working crochet stitches in a circle (called working in the round) instead of in rows opens up new possibilities. Many crocheted shapes are made in the round, including blanket squares, hexagons, and flowers (see pp.161–5). Instead of a foundation chain, circles start with a ring. Here are two popular methods; crochet patterns usually tell you which one to use.

Starting with a magic adjustable ring

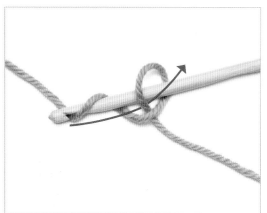

1 A "magic" ring allows you to adjust the size of the centre hole. Form a circle of yarn and draw the yarn through it (as if starting a slip knot, see p.26).

Loop on the hook. Yrh is being drawn through to make I chain

Open circle of yarn

2 Leave the circle of yarn open, then make chain stitches to the height of your pattern stitch. To start a round of double crochet stitches, as shown here, make 1 chain.

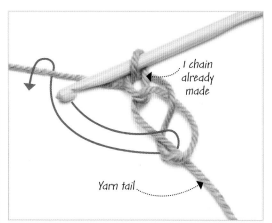

I chain already made

Yarn tail

3 Work the first round of stitches into the centre of the ring and over the yarn tail, as shown by the large arrow.

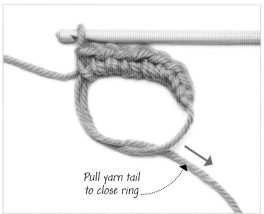

Pull yarn tail to close ring

4 When all stitches of the first round are worked into the ring, pull the yarn tail to close the ring. Then continue with the pattern.

Starting with a chain ring

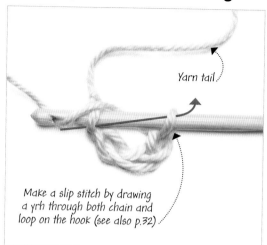

Yarn tail

Make a slip stitch by drawing a yrh through both chain and loop on the hook (see also p.32)

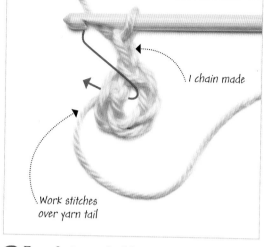

I chain made

Work stitches over yarn tail

1 Many patterns start with chain rings. Start with 4 ch (or as many as your pattern specifies). Form the chains into a foundation ring by working a slip stitch into the last chain from the hook, as shown by the large arrow.

2 For a first round of double crochet, as shown here, start with 1 chain. Then lay the yarn tail around the top of the chain and start working stitches through the centre of the ring and over the yarn tail to secure it.

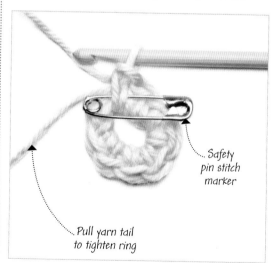

Safety pin stitch marker

Pull yarn tail to tighten ring

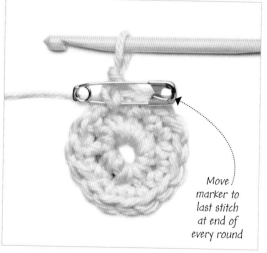

Move marker to last stitch at end of every round

3 When all double crochet stitches of the first round are complete, mark the last stitch of the round with a stitch marker, as shown. Pull the yarn tail to tighten the centre hole and clip it off close to the crochet.

4 In the second round, 2 dc is worked into each dc of the first round. The extra stitches create the curved edge of the circle. Try the Coasters project on page 80 to practise a full pattern for a flat circle.

Make a Set of Coasters

Made with garden string, these double crochet coasters
have a rustic charm. The simple circle pattern can be
worked with a variety of yarns and thicknesses – crochet
as many rounds as you need to get the size you desire.

Instructions

Yarn

You can use any chunky weight yarn. Here we have used cotton twine and jute twine, each about 50m/54yd

A: Cotton twine x 1 ball
B: Jute twine x 1 ball

Cotton twine x 1

Jute twine x 1

Hook Size

6mm

6mm hook

Notions

Stitch marker

Size

11.5cm (4½in) diameter

Special Abbreviations

2 dc in next dc

Work two complete dc into the same stitch. This is known as making an "increase" because it will increase the number of stitches in the round (see also p.90).

Pattern

Single Colour Coasters (make 2)

With yarn A, make 4 ch and join with a ss in first ch to form a ring.
Round 1 (RS) 1 ch, 8 dc in ring. Do not turn at the end of the round, but continue working in a spiral, with the right side (RS) always facing. (8sts)
Note: Keep count of stitches by placing a stitch marker on the last stitch of each round. There are no turning chains in this pattern.
Round 2 2 dc in each dc. (16sts)
Round 3 *1 dc in next dc, 2 dc in next dc; rep from * to end. (24sts)
Round 4 1 dc in each dc.
Round 5 *1 dc in next dc, 2 dc in next dc; rep from * to end. (36sts)
Round 6 Rep round 4.
Work 1 ss in next dc, fasten off, and weave in ends.

Two-colour Coasters (make 2)

Follow pattern for Single Colour Coaster, but change to yarn B for rounds 3 and 4, changing colour on the last yrh of last stitch of round 2. Carry yarn A at the back of the work (see below). Switch back to yarn A for rounds 5 and 6. Work 1 ss in next dc, fasten off, and weave in ends.

Carrying colours

The white twine (yarn A) is carried on the back. To do this, wrap yarn A around the new colour (B), moving it to the back, before starting the round in yarn B. Continue wrapping the non-working yarn for each round until it is needed again. (See p.39.)

11-round Cotton Coasters

Working with rough twine can be hard on the hands, so if you'd prefer to work with DK cotton yarn and a 4mm hook, continue with the pattern to make an 11-round coaster.
Round 7 *1 dc in each of next 2 dc, 2 dc in next dc; rep from * to end. (48sts)
Round 8 Rep round 4.
Round 9 *1 dc in each of next 3 dc, 2 dc in next dc; rep from * to end. (60sts)
Round 10 Rep round 4.
Round 11 1 dc in each of first 2 dc, 2 dc in next dc, *1 dc in each of next 4 dc, 2 dc in next dc; rep from *, ending with 1 dc in each of last 2 dc. (72sts)
Work 1 ss in next dc, fasten off, and weave in ends.
To make a bigger circle, continue on this way, adding 12 extra dc stitches in every alternate round (by working one more stitch between stitches) and altering the position of the first increase on every increase round.

Make a Round Cushion

This pretty cushion features concentric stripes worked in rounds of treble crochet. It is made from two circles stitched together around the edges. Follow this colour scheme of cool blues, or choose your own palette of four toning shades.

Instructions

Yarn

You can use any Aran weight yarn. Here we have used Debbie Bliss Cashmerino Aran 50g (90m/98yd) in 4 colours.

A: 208 Cobalt x 2 balls

B: 101 Ecru x 1 ball

C: 205 Denim x 1 ball

D: 046 Heather x 1 ball

Hook Size

5mm hook

Notions

Round cushion pad, 35cm (14in) diameter

Size

35cm (14in) diameter

208 Cobalt x 2 **101 Ecru x 1** **205 Denim x 1** **046 Heather x 1**

5mm hook

Pattern

Cushion Front

With yarn A, make 4 ch, work 11 tr in 4th ch from hook, ss in top of 3-chain to join. (12sts)

Round 1 3 ch, 1 tr in same st. *2 tr in next st; rep from * to end, ss in top of 3-ch to join. (24sts)

Round 2 3 ch, 2 tr in next st. *1 tr in next st, 2 tr in next st; rep from * to end, ss in top of first 3-ch to join. (36sts)

Change to yarn B.

Round 3 3 ch, 1 tr in next st, 2 tr in next st. *1 tr in each of next 2 sts, 2 tr in next st; rep from * to end, ss in top of first 3-ch to join. (48sts).

Change to yarn C.

Round 4 3 ch, 1 tr in each of next 2 sts, 2 tr in next st. *1 tr in each of next 3 sts, 2 tr in next st; rep from * to end, ss in top of first 3-ch to join. (60sts)

Change to yarn D.

Round 5 3 ch, 1 tr in each of next 3 sts, 2 tr in next st. *1 tr in each

of next 4 sts, 2 tr in next st; rep from * to end, ss in top of first 3-ch to join. (72sts)

Change to yarn A.

Round 6 3 ch, 1 tr in each of next 4 sts, 2 tr in next st. *1 tr in each of next 5 sts, 2 tr in next st; rep from * to end, ss in top of first 3-ch to join. (84sts)

Change to yarn B.

Continue in this way, working one additional single tr between increases per round and changing colour in this order every round, to 132 sts, ending with yarn B. Work one further round in pattern in yarn B. (144sts)

Fasten off yarn.

Cushion Back

Work one more cushion side in the same way, but worked entirely in yarn A.

Finishing

Block pieces lightly (see p.103). Sew the two pieces together around circumference, trapping cushion pad inside.

Tip Instead of starting with a ring of chain stitches, in this pattern the first round of 12 trebles (formed of 3 ch, 11 tr) is worked into a single chain stitch, which helps to avoid creating a large hole in the centre of the circle.

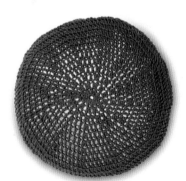

Cushion back

The back of the cushion is made to the same pattern as the front, but in a single colour.

How to **Make Granny Squares**

The granny square (also called an afghan square), is probably the most well-known crochet pattern. For beginners, granny squares are brilliant for practising treble crochet, working in the round, and changing colours. Try making some squares with leftover yarn, and when you have made several you can sew them together into a blanket.

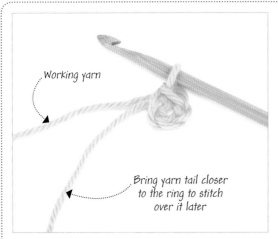

Working yarn

Bring yarn tail closer to the ring to stitch over it later

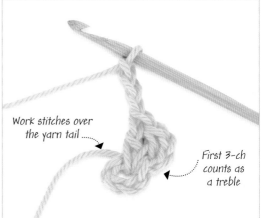

Work stitches over the yarn tail

First 3-ch counts as a treble

1 Start by making a chain-stitch foundation ring. Make 6 ch, then work a slip stitch in the first chain to join the chains into a small foundation ring.

2 For the first round, make 3 chains, work 2 trebles into the ring, and make 3 more chains. Then *work 3 trebles into the ring and 3 chains. Repeat from * two more times.

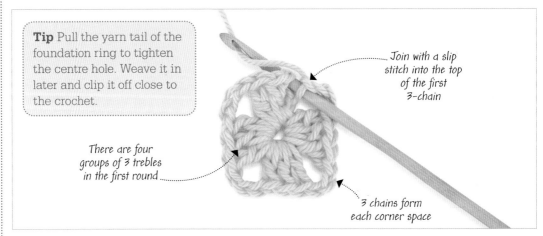

Tip Pull the yarn tail of the foundation ring to tighten the centre hole. Weave it in later and clip it off close to the crochet.

Join with a slip stitch into the top of the first 3-chain

There are four groups of 3 trebles in the first round

3 chains form each corner space

3 Join the round with a slip stitch into the top of the first 3-ch in the round. For a multicoloured motif, fasten off the yarn and join in a new colour for this and each following round. Cut the old yarn and weave it in; join the new colour into any 3-chain corner space.

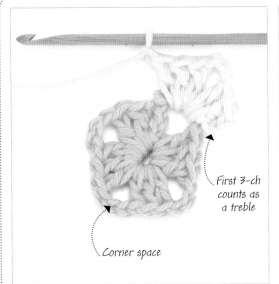

First 3-ch counts as a treble

Corner space

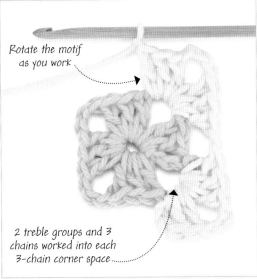

Rotate the motif as you work

2 treble groups and 3 chains worked into each 3-chain corner space

4 Begin the second round with the new colour. Make 3 chains, then work 2 trebles, 3 chains, and 3 trebles into the same corner space. This forms the first corner of round 2.

5 *Chain 1, then work 3 trebles, 3 chains, and 3 trebles into the next corner space. Repeat from * twice more, then chain 1. Join with a slip stitch into the top of the first 3-ch.

Tip In round 3, you'll begin to see that granny squares are made of groups of trebles, with chains to bridge the gaps between each group. Once you know how to work a straight edge and how to work a corner, it is easy to continue the pattern.

1 treble group worked into 1-chain space

1-chain spaces were formed in second round on straight edges

6 For the third round, join the new colour in any 3-chain corner space. Chain 3, then work 2 trebles, 3 chains, and 3 trebles into the same corner space. Chain 1, and work 3 trebles into the next chain space (which is a 1-chain space on the straight edge).

7 *Chain 1, then work 3 trebles, 3 chains, and 3 trebles all in the next 3-chain space for the corner. Chain 1 and work 3 trebles into the next 1-chain space.

8 Repeat from *, until all the chain spaces of the round are filled. To finish the round, chain 1 and join the round with a slip stitch into the top of the first 3-ch.

A finished 3-round granny square

Pattern formed by groups of treble crochet stitches

The square shape made in the round is even on all sides

Each round increases by four more treble groups

How to **Join Colours in Granny Squares**

To start a new colour at the beginning of a granny square round, the most secure method is to fasten off the old colour and join in the new colour with a slip stitch. Join the new yarn in a different corner each time to prevent warping in one corner of the granny square.

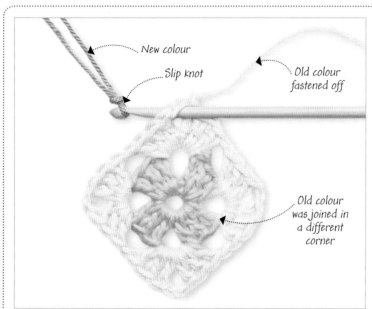

New colour

Slip knot

Old colour fastened off

Old colour was joined in a different corner

1 Make a slip knot with the new colour. Insert the hook at the specified position, place the slip knot on the hook, yrh, and draw the yarn through the loop on the hook. This completes the slip stitch that secures the new yarn to the corner of the square.

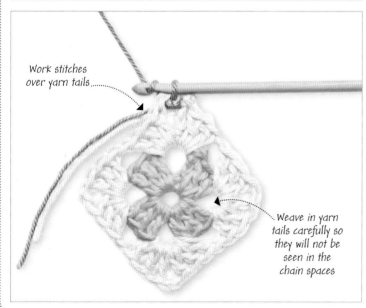

Work stitches over yarn tails

Weave in yarn tails carefully so they will not be seen in the chain spaces

2 Start the new round with the specified number of chains. Work the stitches of the round over both yarn tails (the new colour and the old colour) so that there will be fewer ends to weave in later. To reduce bulk, start the new colour in a different place for each round.

Make a Baby's Blanket

Restful colours and a warm, soft yarn make this a beautiful
first blanket for a baby. It is made as one large granny
square so there are no pieces to join together – just weave
in the ends and finish with a simple border.

Instructions

Yarn

You can use any lightweight DK yarn. Here we have used Debbie Bliss Baby Cashmerino 50g (125m/137yd) in 4 colours

A: 340071 Pool x 2 balls
B: 340101 Ecru x 3 balls
C: 340001 Primrose x 2 balls
D: 340026 Duck egg x 2 balls

Hook Size

3.5mm hook

Size

70cm (27½in) x 70cm (27½in)

340071 Pool x 2

340101 Ecru x 3

340001 Primrose x 2

340026 Duck Egg x 2

3.5mm hook

Pattern
Blanket

With yarn A, make 6 ch, ss in first ch to form a ring. Work with RS facing.

Round 1 3 ch (counts as first tr), 2 tr in ring, 3 ch, *3 tr in ring, 3 ch. Rep from * twice, ss in top of first 3-ch to join.

Round 2 1 ss in each of next 3 sts to reach corner sp.
3 ch (counts as first tr), (2 tr, 3 ch, 3 tr) in same corner sp, *1 ch, (3 tr, 3 ch, 3 tr) in next corner sp, rep from * twice, 1 ch, ss in first 3-ch to join. Fasten off yarn A.

Round 3 Join yarn B into any corner sp (choosing a different sp from where yarn A fastened off). 3 ch (counts as first tr), (2 tr, 3 ch, 3 tr) in same corner sp, 1 ch, 3 tr in next ch sp, 1 ch, *(3 tr, 3 ch, 3 tr) in next corner sp; 1 ch, 3 tr in next ch sp, 1 ch. Rep from * twice, ss in first 3-ch to join.

Round 4 1 ss in each of next 3 sts to reach corner sp.
3 ch (counts as first tr), (2 tr, 3 ch, 3 tr) in each ch sp to corner, 1 ch, *(3 tr,

3ch, 3tr) in corner sp; (1 ch, 3 tr) in each ch sp to corner, 1 ch. Rep from * twice, ss in first 3-ch to join. Fasten off yarn B.
Continue working each round as round 4. Sample blanket is made with 32 more rounds after round 4, with colour changing every two

rounds in this sequence: C, B, D, B, A, B, C, B, D, B, A, B, C, B, D, B.

Edging

Join yarn A in any tr. 1 ch, 1 dc in top of each st around entire blanket, ss in top of first ch to join. Fasten off. Weave in all ends.

Edging stitches

Work the edging stitches under both strands of the "V" of each stitch, including the 3 chains in the corners.

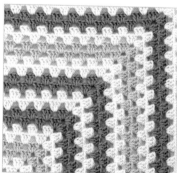

Colour scheme

White stripes between each stronger colour refresh the sequence. The edging matches that of the first two rounds.

How to **Work Double Crochet Increases**

Crochet is shaped by increasing or decreasing the number of stitches in each round or row. You have encountered increases before when crocheting flat circles – they are simply two or three stitches made in the same place. Increases widen the crocheted piece and they can be used on rows as well as rounds, as shown here on double crochet rows.

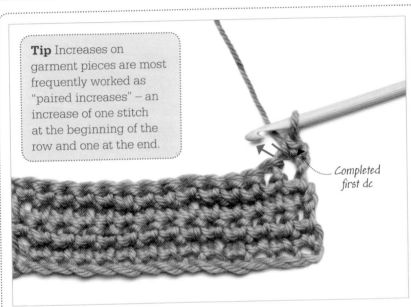

Tip Increases on garment pieces are most frequently worked as "paired increases" – an increase of one stitch at the beginning of the row and one at the end.

Completed *first dc*

1 To increase one stitch at the beginning of a row of double crochet, work 1 dc into the first dc in the usual way. Next, insert the hook again into the first dc and work a second dc in the same stitch.

2 dc worked into same stitch

2 This completes the increase. Continue across the row, working 1 dc into each dc in the usual way.

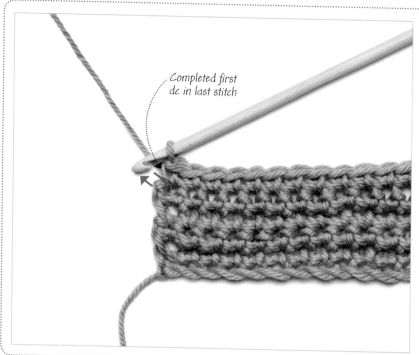

Completed first dc in last stitch

3 At the end of the row, work 1 dc into the last dc of the row in the usual way. Insert the hook again into the last dc of the row and work a second dc into it.

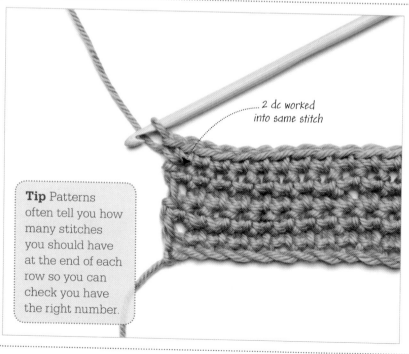

2 dc worked into same stitch

4 This increases one stitch at the end of the row. The new row has 2 more stitches than the previous row.

Tip Patterns often tell you how many stitches you should have at the end of each row so you can check you have the right number.

How to **Work Double Crochet Decreases** (Abbreviation = *dc2tog*)

Decreases are used to narrow a piece of crochet (as opposed to increases which widen the piece). In essence, they are two or three half-completed stitches that are merged into one. Practise decreases until you are comfortable making the stitches. If you keep making paired decreases at both ends of a row you will end up with a triangle.

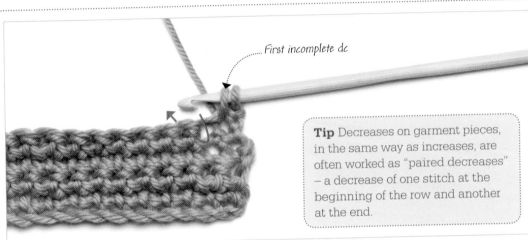

First incomplete dc

Tip Decreases on garment pieces, in the same way as increases, are often worked as "paired decreases" – a decrease of one stitch at the beginning of the row and another at the end.

1 To decrease one stitch at the beginning of a row of double crochet, work up to the last yrh of the first dc in the usual way, but do not

complete the stitch – there are now 2 loops on the hook. Insert the hook through the next stitch as shown and draw a loop through.

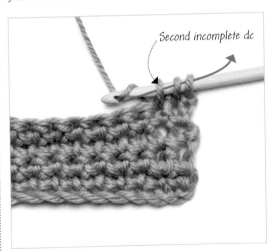

Second incomplete dc

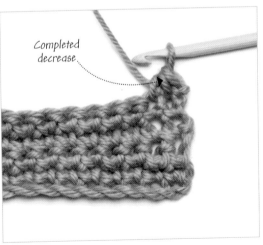

Completed decrease.

2 There are now 3 loops on the hook. Wrap the yarn around the hook and draw it through all 3 loops at once, as shown.

3 This completes the decrease – where there were 2 stitches, there is now only one. Make a complete dc in the next stitch.

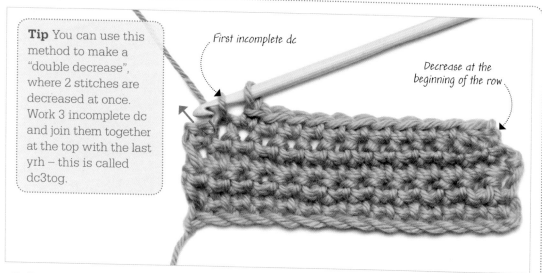

Tip You can use this method to make a "double decrease", where 2 stitches are decreased at once. Work 3 incomplete dc and join them together at the top with the last yrh – this is called dc3tog.

First incomplete dc

Decrease at the beginning of the row

4 Continue across the row, working 1 dc into each dc in the usual way up to the last 2 stitches of the row. At the end of the row, insert the hook through the top of the second to last stitch and draw a loop through – there are now 2 loops on the hook. Insert the hook through the last stitch in the row below as shown by the large arrow and draw a loop through.

Second incomplete dc

Completed decrease

5 There are now 3 loops on the hook. Wrap the yarn around the hook and draw a loop through all 3 loops at once as shown. (The action becomes smoother with practice.) This completes the decrease at the end of the row.

6 The new row has two fewer stitches than the previous row. By crocheting 2 stitches together at each row-end, you've decreased by 1 stitch on each side. (Crocheting 3 stitches together decreases by 2 stitches at a time.)

Make Toy Balls

These delightful little balls are made with small amounts of 4-ply cotton, and stuffed with toy filling so they are soft and squashy. Use a small hook to achieve a tight tension, to form a firm fabric that will hold in the filling.

Instructions

Yarn

You can use any 4-ply mercerized cotton yarn. Here we have used Rowan Siena 4-ply 50g (140m/153yd) in 3 colours

A: 651 White x 1 ball

B: 677 Korma x 1 ball

C: 666 Chilli x 1 ball

651 White x 1

677 Korma x 1

666 Chilli x 1

2mm hook

Hook Size

2mm hook

Notions

Toy stuffing

Size

5cm (2in) diameter

Pattern

Centre Striped Ball

With yarn C, work 6 dc into a magic adjustable ring (see p.78). Pull tail to close.

Round 1 2 dc in each dc to end. (12sts)

Round 2 *1 dc in next dc, 2 dc in next dc; rep from * to end. (18sts)

Round 3 *1 dc in each of next 2 dc, 2 dc in next dc; rep from * to end. (24sts)

Round 4 *1 dc in each of next 3 dc, 2 dc in next dc; rep from * to end. (30sts)

Round 5 *1 dc in each of next 4 dc, 2 dc in next dc; rep from * to end. (36sts)

Round 6 *1 dc in each of next 5 dc, 2 dc in next dc; rep from * to end. (42sts)

Round 7 *1 dc in each of next 6 dc, 2 dc in next dc; rep from * to end. (48sts)

Rounds 8–9 1 dc in each dc to end, finish last dc with yarn A.

Round 10 With yarn A, work 1 dc in each dc to end, finish last dc with yarn B.

Rounds 11–12 With yarn B, work 1 dc in each dc to end, finish last dc of round 12 with yarn A.

Round 13 With yarn A, work 1 dc in each dc to end, finish last dc with yarn C.

Rounds 14–15 With yarn C, work 1 dc in each dc to end.

Round 16 *1 dc in each of next 6 dc, dc2tog; rep from * to end. (42sts)

Round 17 *1 dc in each of next 5 dc, dc2tog; rep from * to end. (36sts)

Round 18 *1 dc in each of next 4 dc, dc2tog; rep from * to end. (30sts)

Round 19 *1 dc in each of next 3 dc, dc2tog; rep from * to end. (24sts)

Round 20 *1 dc in each of next 2 dc, dc2tog; rep from * to end. (18sts)

Round 21 *1 dc in next dc, dc2tog; rep from * to end. (12sts) Stuff very firmly.

Round 22 dc2tog to end. (6sts) Fasten off, leaving a long tail. Use tail to close hole, weave in ends.

All-over Striped Ball

Follow the above pattern, but change the yarn colour at the end of each round, finishing the last st of every round with new colour.

Offset seam

The starting points of the different coloured rounds form an offset seam down the back of the balls.

Tricoloured Block Ball

With yarn B, work 6 dc into a magic adjustable ring (see p.78). Pull tail to close.

Round 1 2 dc in each dc to end. (12sts)

Round 2 *1 dc in next dc, 2 dc in next dc; rep from * to end. (18sts)

Round 3 *1 dc in each of next 2 dc, 2 dc in next dc; rep from * to end. (24sts)

Round 4 *1 dc in each of next 3 dc, 2 dc in next dc; rep from * to end. (30sts)

Round 5 *1 dc in each of next 4 dc, 2 dc in next dc; rep from * to end. (36sts)

Round 6 *1 dc in each of next 5 dc, 2 dc in next dc; rep from * to end. (42sts)

Round 7 *1 dc in each of next 6 dc, 2 dc in next dc; rep from * to end, finish last st with yarn A. (48sts)

Rounds 8–15 With yarn A, work 1 dc in each dc to end, finish last st of round 15 with yarn C.

Round 16 With yarn C, *1 dc in each of next 6 dc, dc2tog; rep from * to end. (42sts)

Rounds 17 *1 dc in each of next 5 dc, dc2tog; rep from * to end. (36sts)

Round 18 *1 dc in each of next 4 dc, dc2tog; rep from * to end. (30sts)

Round 19 *1 dc in each of next 3 dc, dc2tog; rep from * to end. (24sts)

Round 20 *1 dc in each of next 2 dc, dc2tog; rep from * to end. (18sts)

Round 21 *1 dc in next dc, dc2tog; rep from * to end. (12sts) Stuff very firmly.

Round 22 dc2tog to end. (6sts) Fasten off, leaving a long tail. Use tail to close hole, weave in ends.

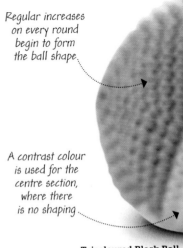

Regular increases on every round begin to form the ball shape.

A contrast colour is used for the centre section, where there is no shaping.

Tricoloured Block Ball

Stuffing round shapes

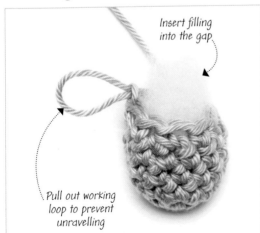

Insert filling into the gap.

Pull out working loop to prevent unravelling

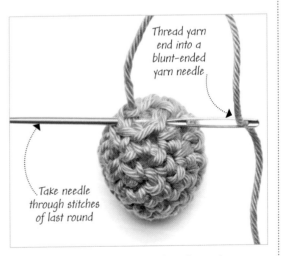

Thread yarn end into a blunt-ended yarn needle

Take needle through stitches of last round

1 When crocheting a ball in one piece, you will need to add the filling before completing the final round. Insert the filling through the gap at the top.

2 Complete the final round and cut the yarn, leaving a long tail. Using a blunt-ended yarn needle, weave the tail through the stitches of the last round to close the gap.

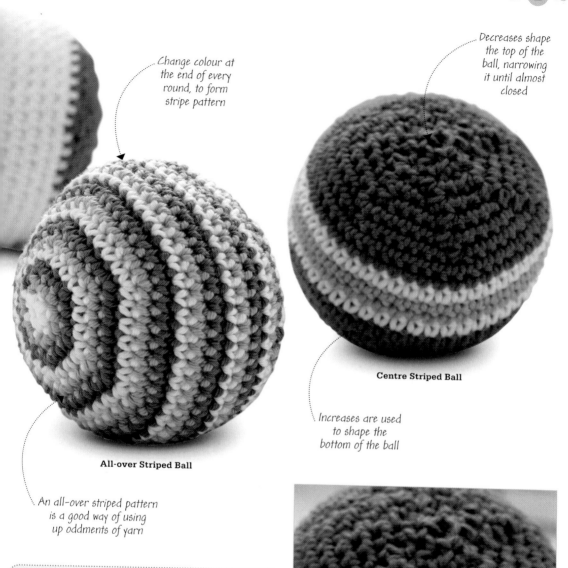

Change colour at the end of every round, to form stripe pattern

Decreases shape the top of the ball, narrowing it until almost closed

Centre Striped Ball

Increases are used to shape the bottom of the ball

All-over Striped Ball

An all-over striped pattern is a good way of using up oddments of yarn

Tip For a neat result, always switch to a new colour by using it to complete the last stitch in the old colour (see p.41). For the all-over striped ball, there is no need to cut the yarn each time you start a new colour: leave all three yarns attached and pick up the colour you need at the end of each round. The yarn strands can be carried across the joins and will be hidden inside the finished ball.

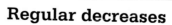

Regular decreases

You can clearly see the regular spacing of the decreases on each round. It is this spacing that gives the ball an even, round shape.

How to **Work Treble Crochet Increases**

Treble crochet increases are worked in the same way as double crochet ones, by making more than one stitch in the same place. This is very simple to do when working in the round, but when treble crochet is worked in rows, keep in mind that each row usually misses a stitch to keep the edges straight. Making a treble in the stitch that is usually missed creates an increase and widens the piece of crochet.

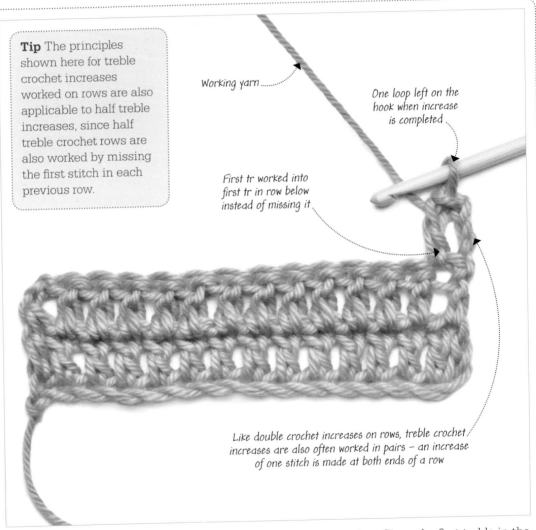

Tip The principles shown here for treble crochet increases worked on rows are also applicable to half treble increases, since half treble crochet rows are also worked by missing the first stitch in each previous row.

Working yarn

One loop left on the hook when increase is completed

First tr worked into first tr in row below instead of missing it

Like double crochet increases on rows, treble crochet increases are also often worked in pairs – an increase of one stitch is made at both ends of a row

1 To increase one stitch at the beginning of a row of treble crochet, first work the turning chain, then work 1 tr into the first tr in the row below. Since the first treble in the row below is usually missed, this creates an increase at the beginning of the row.

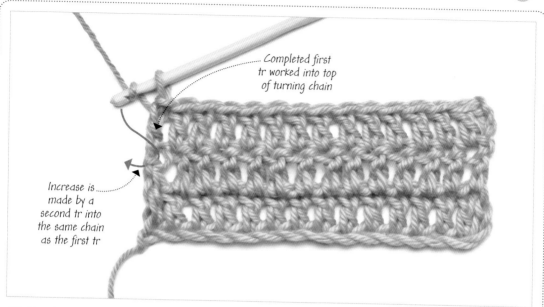

Completed first
tr worked into top
of turning chain

Increase is
made by a
second tr into
the same chain
as the first tr

2 Continue across the row, working 1 tr into each tr in the usual way. At the end of the row, work 1 tr into the top of the turning chain in the row below in the usual way. Then work a second tr into the same turning chain.

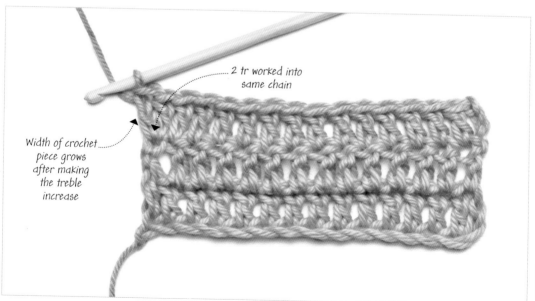

2 tr worked into
same chain

Width of crochet
piece grows
after making
the treble
increase

3 This completes the one stitch increase at the end of the row as shown. The new row has 2 stitches more than the previous row. To make an increase at the start of the next row, chain 3 then work a treble into the first treble in the row below, as shown in Step 1.

How to **Work Treble Crochet Decreases**   (Abbreviation = *tr2tog*)

Decreases have a narrowing effect. Treble crochet decreases, just as double crochet decreases, are two or three incomplete stitches worked together at the top. When you work decreases on treble crochet rows, the turning chain is not included in the decrease, as shown below. The same principles apply to decreases made on half treble crochet rows.

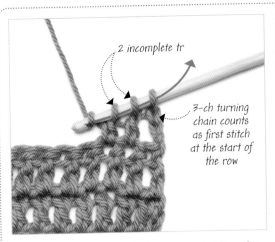

2 incomplete tr

3-ch turning chain counts as first stitch at the start of the row

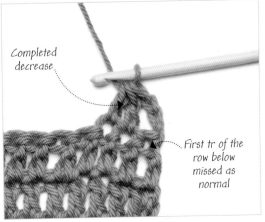

Completed decrease

First tr of the row below missed as normal

1 Work the turning chain as usual. Miss the first tr and work 1 tr in each of the next 2 tr but only up to the last yrh of each stitch. Draw a loop through all 3 loops at once as shown.

2 This completes the decrease – where there were 2 stitches, there is now only one. The turning chain is not counted as part of the treble crochet decrease.

First incomplete tr

Top of turning chain

Tip Making decreases at both the beginning and the end of a row causes the shaping to match on both sides of the crochet piece.

3 Continue across the row in the usual way up to the last tr in the row below. Now work a tr into the last tr but only up to the last yrh. Wrap the yarn around the hook and insert the hook into the top of the turning chain in the row below as shown.

2 incomplete tr

...1 stitch decreased at the beginning of the row

4 Work the tr in the top of the turning chain up to the last yrh of the stitch. There are now 3 loops on the hook. Wrap the yarn around the hook and draw a loop through all 3 loops at once as shown. This completes the decrease at the end of the row.

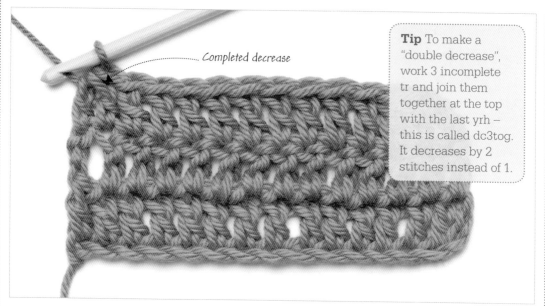

... Completed decrease

Tip To make a "double decrease", work 3 incomplete tr and join them together at the top with the last yrh – this is called dc3tog. It decreases by 2 stitches instead of 1.

5 The new row has two fewer stitches than the previous row. (The turning chain counts as a treble crochet stitch.) By crocheting 2 stitches together at each row-end, you've decreased the number of stitches by 1 stitch on each side.

How to **Measure Tension**

If the final size of the crochet piece is important, always crochet a swatch and measure it before starting the project to check that you achieve the tension (stitch size) stated in the pattern, otherwise your finished item could be too large or too small. Use the same yarn and hook required for the pattern.

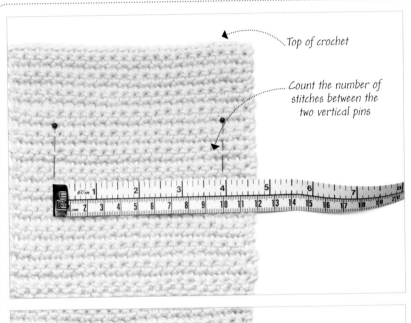

Top of crochet

Count the number of stitches between the two vertical pins

1 Make the foundation chain longer than stated in the tension guide – so if there are 22sts to 10cm (4in), make 28–30 chains plus extra for the stitch height (see p.66). Crochet in rows until you have a square. Mark 10cm (4in) across the centre with pins and count the number of stitches between the two pins.

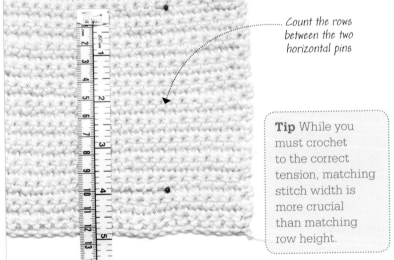

Count the rows between the two horizontal pins

2 Count the number of rows to 10cm (4in) in a similar way. If you have fewer stitches and rows than you should, try again with a smaller hook size; if you have more, change to a larger hook size. Use the hook size that best matches the correct tension.

Tip While you must crochet to the correct tension, matching stitch width is more crucial than matching row height.

How to **Block Crochet Pieces**

Blocking is a process of gentle stretching that perfects the shape and size of your finished crochet pieces. This simple technique benefits many crochet projects, especially if there are pieces that will be joined together and therefore need to be the same size. Check the yarn's care instructions before choosing which method to use.

Wet blocking

If your yarn will allow it, wet blocking is the best way to even out a piece of crochet. Wet the pieces in a sink full of lukewarm water. Then squeeze out the water and roll the crochet in a towel to remove excess dampness. Smooth the crochet into shape right-side down on layers of dry towels covered with a sheet, pinning at intervals. Add as many pins as is necessary to refine the shape. Do not move the crochet until it is completely dry.

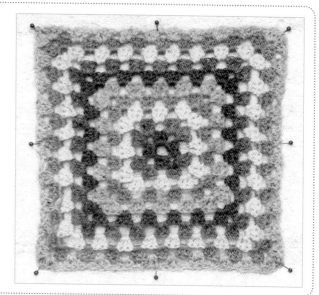

Steam blocking

For a speedier process you may prefer steam blocking (if your yarn label allows it). First, pin the crochet right-side down into the correct shape. Then steam the crochet gently using a clean damp cloth, but barely touching the cloth with the iron. Never rest the weight of an iron on your crochet or it will flatten the texture. Leave the steamed piece to dry fully before unpinning it.

Make a Chevron Cushion

This fabulous zigzag design is created by alternating increases with decreases formed by missed stitches. The cushion cover is made in one piece and stitched up the sides, with the final rows forming an attractive buttoned opening across the centre.

Instructions

Yarn

You can use any DK weight yarn.
Here we have used:
A: Sirdar Click DK 50g
(150m/164yd) in
191 Duck Egg x 2 balls
B: Sirdar Country Style DK 50g
(155m/170yd) in
602 Soft Teal x 1 ball

Hook Size

4mm hook

Notions

Cushion pad 40cm x 30cm
(16in x 12in)
15mm (½in) buttons x 5

Size

40cm x 30cm (16in x 12in)

Pattern

Cushion

With yarn B, make 81 ch.
Row 1 1 dc in 2nd ch from hook,
1 dc in each ch to end, turn. (80sts)
Rows 2–3 1 ch, 2 dc in next st, 1
dc in each of next 7 sts, miss next
2 sts, 1 dc in each of next 7 sts, *2
dc in each of next 2 sts, 1 dc in
each of next 7 sts, miss next 2 sts,
1 dc in each of next 7 sts; rep from
* to last st, 2 dc in last st. Turn.
Change to yarn A.
Rows 4–6 2 ch, 2 htr in next st, 1
htr in each of next 7 sts, miss next
2 sts, 1 htr in each of next 7 sts,
*2 htr in each of next 2 sts, 1 htr in
each of next 7 sts, miss next 2 sts,
1 htr in each of next 7sts; rep from
* to last st, 2 htr in last st. Turn.
Change to yarn B.
Row 7 1 ch, 2 dc in next st, 1 dc
in each of next 7 sts, miss next 2
sts, 1 dc in each of next 7 sts, *2 dc
in each of next 2 sts, 1 dc in each
of next 7 sts, miss next 2 sts, 1 dc
in each of next 7 sts; rep from * to

 191 Duck Egg x 2

 602 Soft Teal x 1

4mm hook

last st, 2 dc in last st. Turn.
Change to yarn A.
Rep rows 4–7 until work measures
approximately 70cm (28in), or
desired length – long enough to fit
comfortably around the cushion
pad with an overlap.
End with a row 7, then rep row
7 twice more in yarn B.
Fasten off.

Finishing

Block piece lightly to shape (see
p.103), then wrap around cushion
pad, with an overlap halfway
down back of pad. Ensure top
edge of piece, with 5 complete
points, is on top, overlapping
bottom of piece. Sew up bottom
two side seams of cushion, then
sew down top two side seams,
overlapping bottom seam. Fasten
middle flap of cushion by sewing

buttons on bottom edge of piece,
corresponding to decrease holes
made in htr row (yarn A), as shown
in the photograph. Fasten buttons
and weave in all ends.

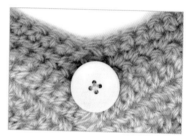

Buttons

Stitch buttons to the bottom
layer of the cushion cover at
the bottom of each "V" in the
zigzag pattern.

Cover edge

The stitch pattern forms a neat zigzag edge to the cushion cover.
The buttons are simply pushed through holes between stitches.

Make a Baby's Hat

This cute, quirky hat would suit a baby girl or boy. Made in one piece, crocheted in the round, the earflaps are then added to the lower edge, while the "ears" are made separately and stitched in place.

Instructions

Yarn
You can use any lightweight DK wool or wool blend yarn. We have used Debbie Bliss Baby Cashmerino 50g (125m/137yd) in 2 colours
A: 032 Sky x 1 ball
B: 064 Mink x 1 ball

032 Sky x 1   **064 Mink x 1**

3.75mm hook

3mm hook

Hook Size
A: 3.75mm hook
B: 3mm hook

Notions
Stitch marker

Tension
17 htr to 10cm (4in)

Size
To fit a baby aged 9–12 months

Special Notes
Crab stitch: Work dc from left to right, instead of right to left. (Left-handed crocheters will work right to left.) After completing a round of double crochet, do not turn work.
1 ch, *insert hook into next stitch to the right (not in the stitch just completed, but the next one), draw a loop through, yrh and pull through both loops on the hook; rep from * to end.

Pattern
Hat Crown
With 3.75mm hook and yarn A, make 3 ch, 8 htr into 3rd ch from hook, ss in first htr to join. (8sts)
Round 1 2 ch, 1 htr in same st. 2 htr in each htr to end, ss in top of 2-ch to join. (16sts)
Round 2 2 ch, 1 htr in same st. *1 htr in next st, 2 htr in next st; rep from * to end, ss in top of 2-ch to join. (24sts)
Round 3 2 ch, 1 htr in same st,

2 htr in next st. *1 htr in each of next 2 sts, 2 htr in next st; rep from * to end, ss in top of 2-ch to join. (32sts)
Round 4 2 ch, 1 htr in each of next 2 sts, 2 htr in next st. *1 htr in each of next 3 sts, 2 htr in next st; rep from * to end, ss in top of 2-ch to join. (40sts)
Round 5 2 ch, 1 htr in each of next 3 sts, 2 htr in next st. *1 htr in each of next 4 sts, 2 htr in next st; rep from * to end, ss in top of 2-ch to join. (48sts)
Continue in this way, working an additional 1 htr between each increase per round, until there are 72sts.
Work one round straight.
Next round 2 ch, 1 htr in each of next 7 sts, 2 htr in next st. *1 htr in each of next 8 sts, 2 htr in next st; rep from * to end, ss in top of 2-ch to join. (80sts)
Work straight without increasing for approximately 8cm (3in).

Earflaps
Rows 1–2 2 ch, 1 htr in each of next 14 sts, turn. (15sts)
Row 3 2 ch, htr2tog, 1 htr in each st to last 3 sts, htr2tog, 1 htr

in last st, turn. (13sts)
Rep last row until there are 5 sts.
Fasten off yarn.
Rejoin yarn to lower edge, 20 sts to the left from first earflap.
Work second earflap to match the first.
Fasten off yarn A.

Edging
Attach yarn B to any st along lower edge. Work 1 ch, then work evenly in dc around entire edge, including earflaps, join with ss in first dc. Do not turn, but work back around in the other direction in using crab stitch to create a corded edge. (See Special Notes.)
Fasten off yarn B and weave in ends.

Ears (make 2 in yarn A and 2 in yarn B)
Using 3mm hook, make 2 ch, 6 dc into 2nd ch from hook, ss in first dc to join. (6sts)
Round 1 1 ch, 2 dc in each dc to end, do not join. (12sts)
Round 2 *1 dc in next dc, 2 dc in next dc, rep from * to end, do not join. (18sts)
Round 3 *1 dc in each of next

2 dc, 2 dc in next dc, rep from * to end, ss in top of first dc to join. (24sts)

Round 4 1 ch, *1 dc in each of next 3 dc, 2 dc in next dc, rep from * to end, ss in top of first dc to join. (30sts)

Finishing

Block all pieces lightly (see p.103).
Sew each yarn B ear piece to a yarn A ear piece, with wrong sides facing each other and yarn B at front.
Sew one completed ear to either side of hat crown, above earflaps.

> **Tip** The ears are worked partly in a spiral (without turning chains) and partly in complete rounds (with turning chains). Place a stitch marker in the first stitch of each round, to help keep track.

Ear

Two layers of spiral rounds are joined together to form each ear. The ears are attached directly to the hat crown.

Corded Edging

Crab stitch – sometimes called "reverse double crochet" – forms a neat corded edge.

Regular increases form a rounded crown

Ears are made separately and stitched in place

The main part
of the hat is
crocheted in
rounds

The earflaps are
made by working
in rows

This neat edge is
made from one row
of double crochet, then
a row of crab stitch

How to **Crochet Tubes**

Crocheting in a tube or cyclinder shape begins with a long foundation chain that is joined to form a ring. The first round of stitches is worked into the chains around this ring. The easiest of all crochet cylinders is double crochet worked in a spiral without turning chains. Stitches taller than double crochet do need chains in each round (see pp.112–3).

Starting a tube

Make sure the chain is not twisted

Tip Unlike the method for flat circles, the stitches for crochet tubes are worked into chain stitches of the ring, and not into the chain space inside the ring.

Completed slip stitch join

Yarn tail will be darned in later, not stitched over

1 Start the crochet tube with the length of chain specified in your crochet pattern. This length determines the circumference of your tube. Then insert the hook through the chain furthest from the hook.

2 Draw a loop through the chain and at the same time through the loop on the hook to complete the slip stitch. This joins the length of chain into a ring. Work the first and following rounds as directed in your pattern.

Double crochet spiral tube

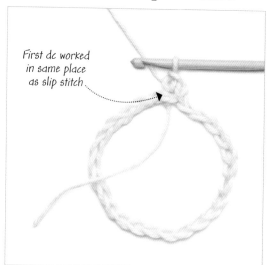

First dc worked in same place as slip stitch

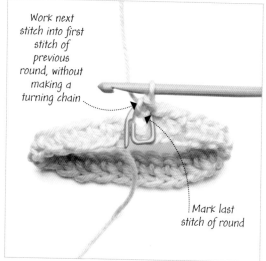

Work next stitch into first stitch of previous round, without making a turning chain

Mark last stitch of round

1 Make the foundation ring and work one chain. Work the first double crochet into the same place as the slip stitch. Then work 1 dc into each of the chains of the ring.

2 Use a stitch marker to keep track of where the rounds begin and end. To begin the second round, work the next stitch into the first stitch of the previous round.

Move marker up at end of each round

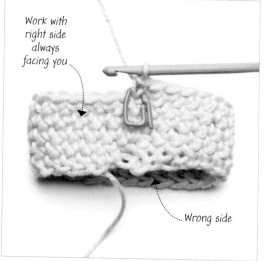

Work with right side always facing you

Wrong side

3 Work 1 dc in each dc in the round below, making sure the right side is facing you. At the end of the round, move the marker up onto the last stitch of this round.

4 Continue round and round in the same way until the tube is the required length. As the spiral grows, you'll notice the start of the round moves gradually to the right.

Treble crochet tube without turns

3 chains count as first stitch of round

Join with a slip stitch to top of 3 chains

Right side

Wrong side

1 This method works a treble crochet tube without turns, with the right side of the work always facing. Begin with 3 chains. Work 1 tr into the next chain and into each of the remaining chains around the ring.

2 At the end of the round, join the last stitch to the top of the 3-chain turning chain with a slip stitch. (Remember to count stitches after finishing the round to check that you have the correct number.)

First treble of each round worked in the chain next to the turning chain

3 chains count as first stitch

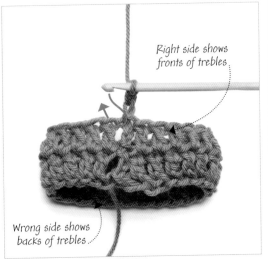

Right side shows fronts of trebles

Wrong side shows backs of trebles

3 Start the second round with 3 chains. There is no need to mark the end of the round with a stitch marker, as the turning chain shows where each round begins.

4 At the end of the second round, join the last stitch to the top of the turning chain with a slip stitch. Continue in the same way, beginning all following rounds with 3 chains.

Treble crochet tube with turns

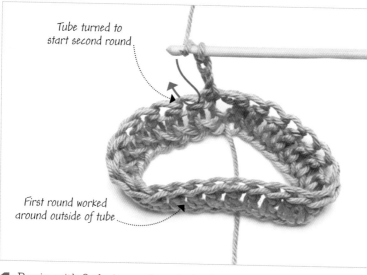

Tube turned to start second round

First round worked around outside of tube

Tip Working a tube with turns results in a fabric that looks like it has been crocheted in rows. This is useful if the tube needs to match crochet worked in rows in other parts of an item.

1 Begin with 3 chains and work the first round of trebles into the foundation chain around the right side of the tube (facing you), as for a tube without turns. Then turn the work, make 3 chains as shown, and complete the round by working around the wrong side of the tube. To finish the round, join the last stitch to the turning chain with a slip stitch.

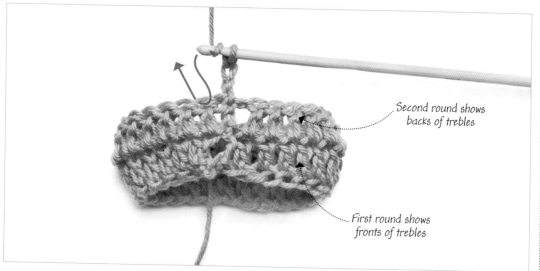

Second round shows backs of trebles

First round shows fronts of trebles

2 To begin the third round, turn the work to the right side and start with 3 chains. Continue in this way, joining the last stitch with a slip stitch to the top of the turning chain at the end of each round, then turning the work to start the next round. The fabric looks just like treble crochet that has been worked in ordinary rows.

Make a Project Basket

This versatile basket begins with a flat circle at the base and continues in a tube-like fashion to shape the sides. A crisp line is formed around the base and the brim foldover by crocheting into the back loop only for one round.

Instructions

Yarn

You can use any DK acrylic yarn. Here we have used Stylecraft Special DK 100g (295m/323yd)
A: 1432 Wisteria x 1 ball
B: 1005 Cream x 1 ball

1432 Wisteria x 1

1005 Cream x 1

Hook Size

4mm hook

4mm hook

Size

13cm x 16 cm (5in x 6 in)

Pattern

Basket

With yarn A, make 2 ch, work 6 dc in 2nd ch from hook.

Round 1 2 dc in each dc to end. (12sts)

Round 2 *1 dc in next dc, 2 dc in next dc; rep from * to end. (18sts)

Round 3 *1 dc in each of next 2 dc, 2 dc in next dc; rep from * to end. (24sts)

Round 4 *1 dc in each of next 3 dc, 2 dc in next dc; rep from * to end. (30sts)

Round 5 *1 dc in each of next 4 dc, 2 dc in next dc; rep from * to end. (36sts)

Round 6 *1 dc in each of next 5 dc, 2 dc in next dc; rep from * to end. (42sts)

Round 7 *1 dc in each of next 6 dc, 2 dc in next dc; rep from * to end. (48sts)

Round 8 *1 dc in each of next 7 dc, 2 dc in next dc; rep from * to end. (54sts)

Round 9 *1 dc in each of next 8 dc, 2 dc in next dc; rep from * to end. (60sts)

Round 10 *1 dc in each of next 9 dc, 2 dc in next dc; rep from * to end. (66sts)

Round 11 *1 dc in each of next 10 dc, 2 dc in next dc; rep from * to end. (72sts)

Round 12 *1 dc in each of next 11 dc, 2 dc in next dc; rep from * to end. (78sts)

Round 13 *1 dc in each of next 12 dc, 2 dc in next dc; rep from * to end. (84sts)

Round 14 *1 dc in each of next 13 dc, 2 dc in next dc; rep from * to end. (90sts)

Round 15 *1 dc in each of next 14 dc, 2 dc in next dc; rep from * to end. (96sts)

Round 16 *1 dc in each of next 15 dc, 2 dc in next dc; rep from * to end. (102sts)
Increases can be stopped earlier for a smaller basket or continued as set for a larger basket.

Round 17 Working into back loops only, 1 dc in each dc to end.

(102sts) Continue working in rounds, inserting hook through both loops (1 dc in each dc to end) until piece measures 13cm (5in) from Round 17, or desired height.

Foldover

Round 1 Working in the front loops only, with yarn B, 1 dc in each dc to end. (102sts)

Round 2 With yarn A, 1 dc in each dc (through both loops) to end. (102sts)

Round 3 With yarn B, 1 dc in each dc (through both loops) to end. (102sts) Rep last 2 rounds once more. Fasten off, weave in ends.

Brim

The decorative brim with three contrasting stripes is crocheted as part of the basket and then folded down.

Bottom

As rounds increase on the bottom of the basket, it begins to look more like a hexagon in shape.

How to **Combine Stitches**

Combining stitches by grouping and merging them allows you to create beautiful stitch patterns and textures. These raised and grouped crochet stitch techniques are easier to do than they first appear, and they can be used to form both solid stitch patterns (see pp.126–129) and lacy, openwork ones (see pp.146–149).

Shells

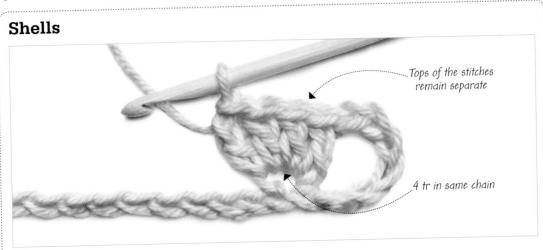

Tops of the stitches remain separate

4 tr in same chain

4-TR SHELL

Shells are probably the most frequently used of all crochet stitch techniques. Usually made with trebles, they are formed by working several stitches into the same stitch or space. Here 4 trebles have been worked into the same chain to form a 4-tr shell.

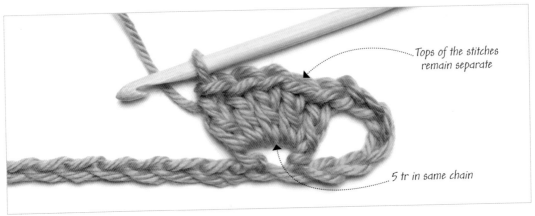

Tops of the stitches remain separate

5 tr in same chain

5-TR SHELL

Here 5 trebles have been worked into the same chain to form a 5-tr shell. Any number of trebles can be used to form a shell, but the most commonly used crochet shells have 2, 3, 4, 5, or 6 stitches. Shells can also be made with half trebles and taller basic stitches.

Clusters

Tip Crocheted clusters look like upside-down shells. They are made by joining the tops of several stitches (each worked into a different stitch below) together to become one.

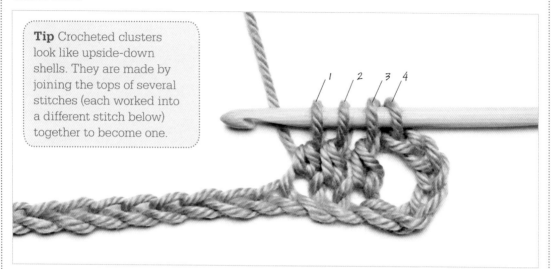

1 To make a 3-tr cluster, work 1 treble up to the last yrh that completes the tr (this forms one incomplete treble stitch). Then work 1 incomplete tr into each of the next 2 stitches in the row below in same way. There are now 4 loops on the hook.

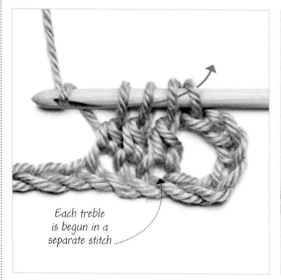

Each treble is begun in a separate stitch

Top of the cluster becomes a single stitch

2 Wrap the yarn around the hook and draw a loop through all 4 loops on the hook. This action completes all of the trebles at the same time and joins them at the top into a single stitch.

3 This completes the 3-tr cluster. Clusters can be made with any number of trebles, but 2, 3, 4, 5, or 6 stitches are most common. Half trebles or taller basic stitches can be used to form clusters as well.

Bobbles

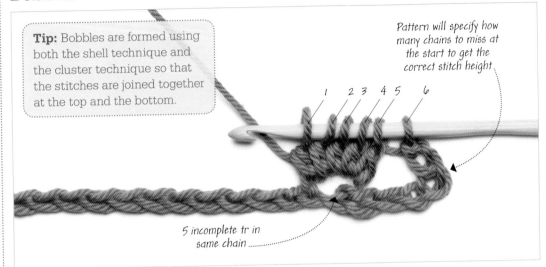

Tip: Bobbles are formed using both the shell technique and the cluster technique so that the stitches are joined together at the top and the bottom.

Pattern will specify how many chains to miss at the start to get the correct stitch height

1 2 3 4 5 6

5 incomplete tr in same chain

1 To work a 5-tr bobble, work 5 incomplete trebles (as for a cluster) into the same stitch (as for a shell). To work the first incomplete treble: yrh, insert the hook into the stitch, yrh again, and draw a loop through the first 2 loops on the hook. Repeat to make four more incomplete trebles in the same stitch. There are now 6 loops on the hook.

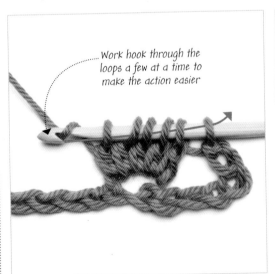

Work hook through the loops a few at a time to make the action easier

2 Wrap the yarn around the hook and draw a loop through all 6 loops on the hook. This completes all of the trebles at the same time and joins them at the top.

Bobble can be pushed out on one side of the work for extra texture

3 Some bobbles are completed with an extra chain, as shown by the large arrow. Bobbles are usually made with 3, 4, or 5 treble stitches. Half treble bobbles are called "puffs".

Popcorns

Start with a group of complete stitches

Insert hook under both strands of the first treble

1 Popcorns are a variation on bobbles, but they are started like shells. To make a 5-tr popcorn, begin by working 5 trebles in the same stitch. Your pattern will specify which stitch to make the popcorn in.

2 Remove the hook from the loop and insert it from front to back through the top of the first treble of the group. Draw the working loop through the top of the first treble as shown by the large arrow.

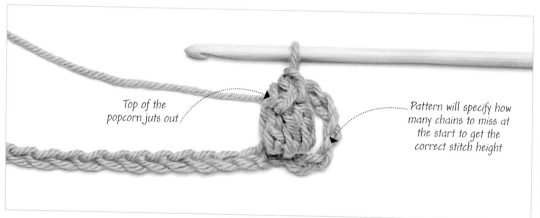

Top of the popcorn juts out

Pattern will specify how many chains to miss at the start to get the correct stitch height

3 This pulls the top of the shell together to form a bobble-type shape. Unlike the top of a bobble, the top of a popcorn sticks out because of the method of construction, creating a bold texture. Popcorns are usually made with 3, 4, or 5 trebles.

Make a Bookmark

This small project is quick to crochet and would make an ideal gift. If you have never used fine crochet cotton and a small steel hook before, you may find the work a bit fiddly to begin with, but the results are worth the effort.

Instructions

Yarn

You can use any 2-ply mercerized cotton yarn. Here we have used DMC Petra 3 100g (280m/306yd) 53837 Purple x 1 ball

Hook Size

1.5mm hook

Size

2cm x 18cm (¾in x 7in)

Pattern

Make 51 ch.

Row 1 1 dc in 2nd ch from hook, 1 dc in each rem ch to end, turn. (50sts)

Rows 2–3 1 ch, 1 dc in each dc to end, turn. (50sts)

Row 4 1 ch, 1 dc in first st, *miss 1 st, 5 tr in next st, miss 1 st, ss in next st; rep from * around entire piece including other side of foundation chain, ending 1 dc in last st, leaving last short side unworked.

Fasten off, weave in ends.

Tassel

Cut 8 strands of yarn twice the length of desired tassel (about 40cm/16in). Insert hook into centre of unworked short side, fold yarn over hook at centre of strands, pull loop through, fold all tails over hook and pull tails through. Trim the ends neatly.

Finishing

Press the bookmark lightly once finished, to flatten it.

53837 Purple x 1

1.5mm hook

Shell Edging

Treble crochet shell edging runs along both sides of the bookmark, creating an attractive symmetrical pattern of half circles.

Tassel

A tassel is surprisingly easy to make. It provides a neat finishing touch and makes it easy to find your place in the book.

Make a Clutch Bag

This elegant little purse is just big enough to hold all your
essentials for an evening out. Using a shiny mercerized
yarn, it is made in rows using the cluster and shell stitch
from page 127, which forms a pretty scalloped edging.

Instructions

Yarn

You can use any DK mercerized cotton yarn. Here we have used Rico Design Essentials Cotton DK 50g (130m/142yd) 016 Lilac x 1 ball

Hook Size

3.5mm hook

Notions

Shell button, approximately 2cm (¾in)

Size

20cm x 10cm (8in x 4in)

Special Notes

Cluster: over next 5 sts, (which include 2 tr, 1 dc, 2 tr), work (yrh and insert hook in next st, yrh and draw a loop through, yrh and draw through first two loops on hook) 5 times (6 loops on hook), yrh and draw through all 6 loops on hook.

Pattern

Make 46 ch.
Row 1 2 tr in 4th ch from hook, miss next 2 ch, 1 dc in next ch, *miss next 2 ch, 5 tr in next ch, miss next 2 ch, 1 dc in next ch; rep from * to last 3 ch, miss next 2 ch, 3 tr in last ch, turn.
Row 2 1 ch, 1 dc in first tr, *2 ch, 1 cluster over next 5 sts, 2 ch, 1 dc in centre tr of 5-tr group; rep from * to end, working last dc of last rep in top of 3-ch at end, turn.
Row 3 3 ch, 2 tr in first dc, miss next 2 ch, 1 dc in next st (top of first cluster), miss next 2 ch, *5 tr in next dc, miss next 2 ch, 1

016 Lilac x 1

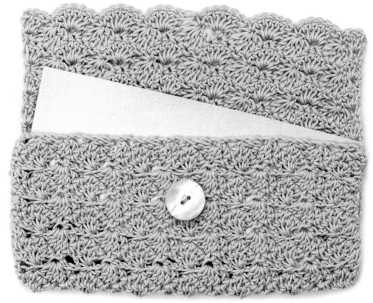

3.5mm hook

dc in next st (top of next cluster); rep from *, ending with 3 tr in last dc, turn.
Rep rows 2 and 3 until piece measures 25cm (10in), ending on a row 3. Fold at 10cm (4in) and sew two sides to form a pocket. Fold top flap over and attach a button (the pattern forms spaces that can be used as buttonholes).

Lining

You may choose to line your clutch with fabric, or place a piece of card inside to help it keep its shape.

How to **Follow Stitch Symbol Diagrams**

Crochet symbol diagrams can be even easier to follow than written patterns because they provide a visual reference of the stitches. Each symbol represents a basic stitch, and is positioned so that its base points to the stitch or chain space it is worked into. Since diagrams show how the pattern is constructed, rows are read back and forth, and rounds are read in a spiral, just as you would crochet them. Symbol diagrams are often used for repeating stitch patterns and motifs.

Crochet stitch symbols

These are the symbols used in this book, but crochet symbols are not universal so always consult the key that accompanies your crochet instructions.

Basic stitches	Special stitches and stitch combinations		Shells, clusters, bobbles, popcorns
○ = ch	= 3-ch, 4-ch, 5-ch picots	⋀ = htr2tog ✕ = 3 dc in same st	= 2-, 3-, 4-, 5-, 6-tr shells (see p.116)
•• = ss	= trtr		
+ = dc	= fptr (front post treble)	⋀ = htr3tog V = 2 htr in same st	= 2-, 3-, 4-, 5-, 6-tr clusters (see p.117)
= qtr	= bptr (back post treble)	⋀ = tr2tog V = 3 htr in same st	
⊤ = htr			= 3-, 4-, 5-tr bobbles (see p.118)
= tr = quintr	✕✕ = dc2tog	⋀ = tr3tog	
= dtr	✕ = dc3tog	✕✕ = 2 dc in same st	= 3-, 4-, 5-tr popcorns (see p.119)

Understanding stitch symbol diagrams

Crochet this swatch of close shells stitch (see also p.126) using the symbol diagram, which starts at the bottom and works upwards, like the crochet itself.

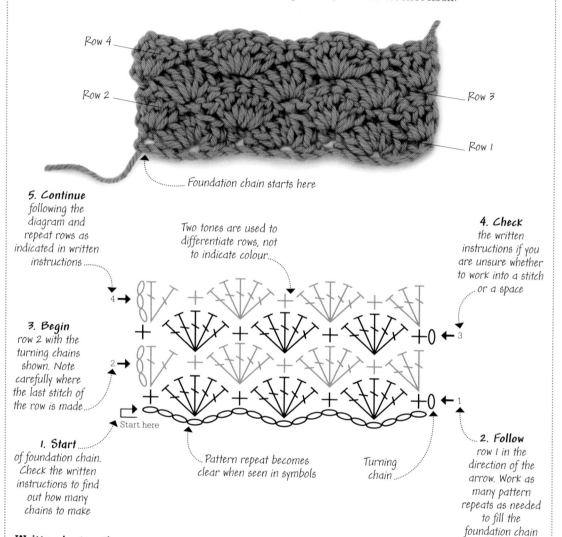

Row 4

Row 2

Row 3

Row 1

.... Foundation chain starts here

5. Continue following the diagram and repeat rows as indicated in written instructions ....

Two tones are used to differentiate rows, not to indicate colour...

4. Check the written instructions if you are unsure whether to work into a stitch ... or a space

3. Begin row 2 with the turning chains shown. Note carefully where the last stitch of the row is made...

1. Start ..... of foundation chain. Check the written instructions to find out how many chains to make

Start here

... Pattern repeat becomes clear when seen in symbols

Turning chain ...

2. Follow row 1 in the direction of the arrow. Work as many pattern repeats as needed to fill the foundation chain

Written instructions

Make a multiple of 6 ch, plus 2 extra.

Row 1 1 dc in 2nd ch from hook, *miss next 2 ch, 5 tr in next ch, miss next 2 ch, 1 dc in next ch; rep from * to end, turn.

Row 2 3 ch (counts as first tr), 2 tr in first dc, *miss next 2 tr, 1 dc in next tr, 5 tr in next dc (between shells); rep from *, ending last rep with 3 tr (instead of 5 tr) in last dc, turn.

Row 3 1 ch (does not count as a st), 1 dc in first tr, *5 tr in next dc (between shells), miss next 2 tr, 1 dc in next tr; rep from *, working last dc in top of 3-ch at end, turn.

Rep rows 2 and 3 to form patt.

Gallery of **Basic Stitch Patterns**

You can create a wealth of interesting patterns with the basic and grouped stitches at your disposal. The stitch patterns in this gallery all create solid (rather than lacy) textures, are easy to work, and quick to memorize after the first few rows. They all look good on both sides of the fabric and would make lovely cushion covers, baby blankets, or throws.

Simple Texture Stitch

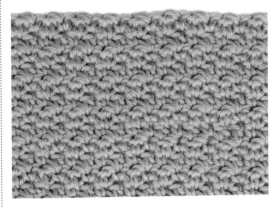
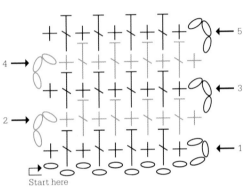

Make a multiple of 2 ch.
Row 1 (RS) 1 dc in 4th ch from hook, *1 tr in next ch, 1 dc in next ch; rep from * to end, turn.
Row 2 3 ch (counts as first tr), miss first dc, *1 dc in next

tr, 1 tr in next dc; rep from *, ending with 1 dc in top of 3-ch at end, turn.
Rep row 2 to form patt.

Close Shells Stitch

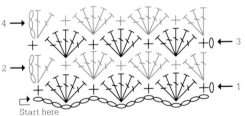

Make a multiple of 6 ch, plus 2 extra.
Row 1 1 dc in 2nd ch from hook, *miss next 2 ch, 5 tr in next ch, miss next 2 ch, 1 dc in next ch; rep from * to end, turn.
Row 2 3 ch (counts as first tr), 2 tr in first dc, *miss next 2 tr, 1 dc in next tr, 5 tr in next dc (between shells); rep

from *, ending last rep with 3 tr (instead of 5 tr) in last dc, turn.
Row 3 1 ch (does not count as a st), 1 dc in first tr, *5 tr in next dc (between shells), miss next 2 tr, 1 dc in next tr; rep from *, working last dc in top of 3-ch at end, turn.
Rep rows 2 and 3 to form patt.

Shells and Chains Stitch

Make a multiple of 6 ch, plus 2 extra.
Row 1 (RS) 1 dc in 2nd ch from hook, *miss next 2 ch, (1 tr, 1 ch, 1 tr, 1 ch, 1 tr) in next ch, miss next 2 ch, 1 dc in next ch; rep from * to end, turn.
Row 2 4 ch (counts as 1 tr and 1-ch sp), 1 tr in first dc, miss next tr, 1 dc in next tr (centre tr of shell), *(1 tr, 1 ch, 1 tr, 1 ch, 1 tr) in next dc (between shells), miss next tr, 1 dc in next tr (centre tr of shell); rep from *, ending with

(1 tr, 1 ch, 1 tr) in last dc, turn.
Row 3 1 ch (does not count as a st), 1 dc in first tr, *(1 tr, 1 ch, 1 tr, 1 ch, 1 tr) all in next dc, miss next tr, 1 dc in next tr (centre tr of shell); rep from *, working last dc of last rep in 3rd of 4-ch made at beg of previous row, turn.
Rep rows 2 and 3 to form patt.

Cluster and Shell Stitch

Note: cluster (also called tr5tog) = over next 5 sts (which include 2 tr, 1 dc, 2 tr) work (yrh and insert hook in next st, yrh and draw a loop through, yrh and draw through first 2 loops on hook) 5 times (6 loops now on hook), yrh and draw through all 6 loops on hook (see p.117).
Make a multiple of 6 ch, plus 4 extra.
Row 1 (RS) 2 tr in 4th ch from hook, miss next 2 ch, 1 dc in next ch, *miss next 2 ch, 5 tr in next ch, miss next 2 ch, 1 dc in next ch; rep from * to last 3 ch, miss next 2 ch, 3 tr in last ch, turn.

Row 2 1 ch (does not count as a st), 1 dc in first tr, *2 ch, 1 cluster over next 5 sts, 2 ch, 1 dc in next tr (centre tr of 5-tr group); rep from *, working last dc of last rep in top of 3-ch at end, turn.
Row 3 3 ch (counts as first tr), 2 tr in first dc, miss next 2 ch, 1 dc in next st (top of first cluster), *5 tr in next dc, miss next 2 ch, 1 dc in next st (top of next cluster); rep from *, ending with 3 tr in last dc, turn.
Rep rows 2 and 3 to form patt.

Simple Bobble Stitch

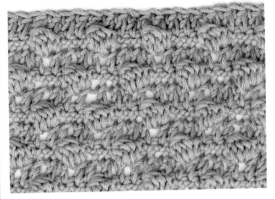

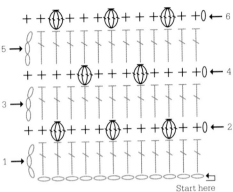

Note: bobble = (yrh and insert hook in specified st, yrh and draw a loop through, yrh and draw through first 2 loops on hook) 4 times all in same st (5 loops now on hook), yrh and draw through all 5 loops on hook (see p.118).
Make a multiple of 4 ch, plus 3 extra.
Row 1 (WS) 1 tr in 4th ch from hook, 1 tr in each of rem ch, turn.
Row 2 (RS) 1 ch (does not count as a st), 1 dc in each of first 2 tr, *1 bobble in next tr, 1 dc in each of next 3 tr; rep from * to last 2 tr, 1 bobble in next tr, 1 dc in next tr, 1 dc in top of 3-ch at end, turn.
Row 3 3 ch (counts as first tr), miss first dc and work 1 tr in each st to end, turn.
Row 4 1 ch (does not count as a st), 1 dc in each of first 4 tr, *1 bobble in next tr, 1 dc in each of next 3 tr; rep from *, ending with 1 dc in top of 3-ch at end, turn.
Row 5 Rep row 3.
Rep rows 2–5 to form patt, ending with a patt row 5.

Popcorn Pattern Stitch

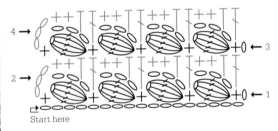

Note: popcorn = 5 tr all in same st, carefully remove loop from hook and insert it through top of first tr of this 5-tr group, pull loop (the one removed from hook) through first tr (see p.119).
Make a multiple of 4 ch, plus 2 extra.
Row 1 (RS) 1 dc in 2nd ch from hook, *3 ch, 1 popcorn in same place as last dc, miss next 3 ch, 1 dc in next ch; rep from * to end, turn.

Row 2 3 ch (counts as first tr), *(2 dc, 1 htr) in next 3-ch sp, 1 tr in next dc; rep from * to end, turn.
Row 3 1 ch (does not count as a st), 1 dc in first tr, *3 ch, 1 popcorn in same place as last dc, miss next 3 sts, 1 dc in next tr; rep from *, working last dc of last rep in top of 3-ch at end, turn.
Rep rows 2 and 3 to form patt.

Simple Puff Stitch

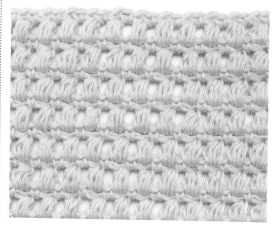

KEY

4-htr puff stitch

Note: puff stitch = (yrh and insert hook in st) 4 times all in same st (9 loops now on hook), yrh and draw through all 9 loops on hook to complete 4-htr puff stitch.
Make a multiple of 2 ch.
Row 1 (RS) 1 dc in 2nd ch from hook, *1 ch, miss next ch, 1 dc in next ch; rep from * to end, turn.
Row 2 2 ch (counts as first htr), 1 puff st in first 1-ch sp, *1 ch, 1 puff st in next 1-ch sp; rep from *, ending with 1 htr in last dc, turn.
Row 3 1 ch (does not count as a st), 1 dc in first htr, *1 ch, 1 dc in next 1-ch sp; rep from *, working last dc of last rep in top of 2-ch at end, turn.
Rep rows 2 and 3 to form patt.

Simple Crossed Stitch

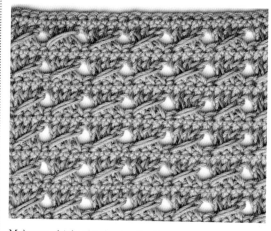

Make a multiple of 4 ch, plus 2 extra.
Row 1 1 dc in 2nd ch from hook, 1 dc in each of rem ch, turn.
Row 2 (RS) 3 ch (counts as first tr), miss first dc, 1 tr in each of next 3 dc, yrh and insert hook from front to back in first dc (the missed dc), yrh and draw a long loop through (extending the loop so that it reaches back to position of work and does not squash 3-tr group just made), (yrh and draw through first 2 loops on hook) twice (called long tr), *miss next dc, 1 tr in each of next 3 dc, 1 long tr in last missed dc; rep from * to last dc, 1 tr in last dc, turn.
Row 3 1 ch (does not count as a st), 1 dc in each tr to end (do not work a dc in 3-ch turning chain), turn.
Rep rows 2 and 3 to form patt.

129

3

Take It Further

Congratulations – you have achieved an excellent base of crochet skills by this point. In this chapter, you'll build on the techniques you already know and hone them further. Create crochet lace using chain loops and combined stitches, make some intricate edgings, move beyond stripes with advanced colourwork techniques, and learn some clever new shaping skills. With your new knowledge, you can tackle projects such as a lacy scarf, a baby's cardigan, a colourful bag, and have the confidence to continue your crochet adventure.

Learn to crochet:

Lacy Scarf
pp.150–151

Patchwork Blanket
pp.166–167

Teddy Bear
pp.182–185

Baby's Shoes
pp.186–187

How to **Work Around The Post**

Treble crochet, and every stitch taller than a treble, has enough space between stitches to work the hook around the body, or post, of the stitches. Working around the post creates a ridged effect, and when crocheted in rows, the ridges create a fabric that imitates knitted ribbing.

Front post treble (Abbreviation = fptr)

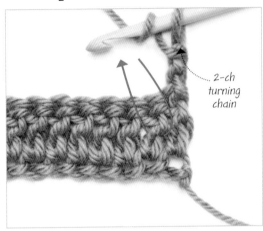

... 2-ch turning chain

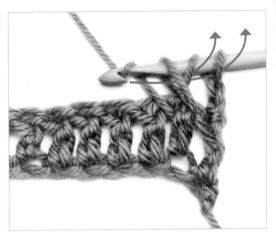

1 Start with a row of trebles. To begin the second row, work 2 chains, yrh, and insert the hook from the front around the post of the second treble, as shown by the large arrow.

2 To complete the treble, yrh and draw a loop through, then (yrh and draw through the first 2 loops on the hook) twice as shown by the two large arrows.

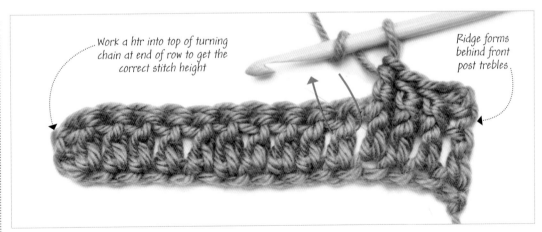

Work a htr into top of turning chain at end of row to get the correct stitch height

Ridge forms behind front post trebles

3 Work a treble around each of the trebles in the row below in the same way, inserting the hook from the front of the work facing you.

At the end of the row, work a half treble into the top of the turning chain. Repeat the second row to form a ridged texture.

Back post treble (Abbreviation = *bptr*)

.... *2-ch turning chain*

1 Start with a row of trebles. To begin the second row, work 2 chains, yrh and insert the hook from the back around the post of the second treble, as shown by the large arrow.

2 To complete the treble, yrh and draw a loop through, then (yrh and draw through the first 2 loops on the hook) twice as shown by the two large arrows.

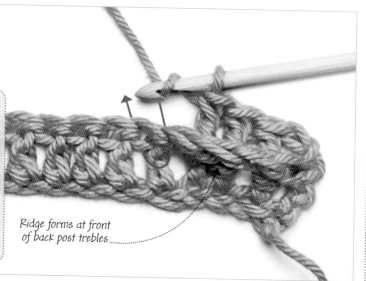

Tip Starting the stitch in a lower position means that the stitch height becomes slightly shorter. As a result both front and back post treble crochet use a 2-ch turning chain instead of a 3-ch one, and finish with each row with a htr.

Ridge forms at front of back post trebles ....

3 Work a treble around each of the trebles in the row below in the same way, inserting the hook from the back of the work facing you.

At the end of the row, work a half treble into the top of the turning chain. Continue the ridged texture by repeating the second row.

Make a Ribbed Scarf

This masculine scarf has a chunky, textured appearance.
It is made by working back and forth in rows using front
post and back post trebles (see pp.132–133), which creates
an appealing "ribbed" fabric.

Instructions

Yarn

You can use any DK wool or wool blend yarn. Here we have used Rowan Colourspun DK 50g (135m/148yd) 276 Semer Water x 4 balls

Hook Size

5mm hook

Size

18cm x 130cm (7in x 51in) or desired length

Special Notes

fptr: front post treble. Yrh and insert hook around the post of next st, taking hook from front to back to front, yrh and pull up a loop, yrh and pull through two loops, yrh and pull through last two loops. (See p.132.)

bptr: back post treble. Yrh and insert hook around the post of next st, taking hook from back to front to back, yrh and pull up a loop, yrh and pull through two loops, yrh and pull through last two loops. (See p.133.)

276 Semer Water x 4

5mm hook

Pattern

Make 34 ch.

Row 1 1 tr in 4th ch from hook, 1 tr in each ch to end, turn. (31sts)

Row 2 2 ch, miss first tr, *fptr around next st, bptr around next st; rep from * to end, htr in top of turning ch at end, turn.

Rep row 2 until piece measures 130cm (51in), or desired length (additional balls of yarn will be required to make scarf longer). Fasten off, weave in ends.

Yarn

The gently variegated yarn used for this project forms subtle stripes when worked back and forth in rows.

Rib stitch

The crochet rib stitch forms deep, textured ridges that help trap heat, making the scarf really warm and cosy.

How to **Crochet Openwork**

Lacy, decorative openwork crochet has an enduring appeal, whether made with fine threads for lace collars, pillow edgings, and tablecloths or with soft wools for shawls, throws, and scarves. These airy lace textures are produced by working chain spaces and chain loops between the basic stitches, as is explained using the examples below and overleaf.

Chain loop mesh

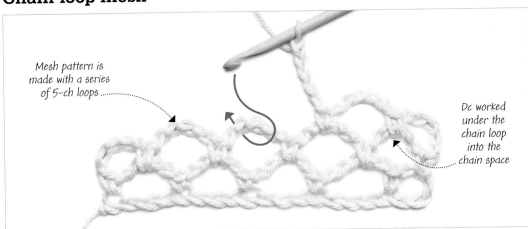

Mesh pattern is made with a series of 5-ch loops .....

Dc worked under the chain loop into the chain space

1 A chain loop mesh (see p.146 for the pattern) is made by joining short lengths of chain called chain loops. After the foundation row, join the 5-chain loops of the following rows to the loops below with a dc worked into the chain spaces under the chain loops.

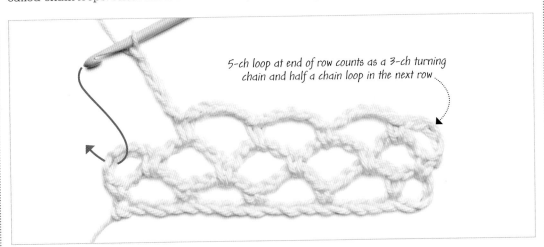

5-ch loop at end of row counts as a 3-ch turning chain and half a chain loop in the next row .....

2 Work the last dc of each row into the space inside the turning chain made at the beginning of the previous row. If you don't, your lace fabric will become narrower.

Shell mesh stitch

Dc at sides of shell secure it to mesh row below

1 The shell mesh stitch pattern (see p.148) is worked into both chain spaces and tops of stitches. Make each shell by working the treble stitches into the top of a dc as shown.

2 Complete each shell with a dc worked into the following chain space. Then work a chain loop and join it to the next chain loop with a dc as shown.

Tip Openwork crochet patterns work up very quickly, which makes them popular for large pieces such as scarves, shawls, and tablecloths.

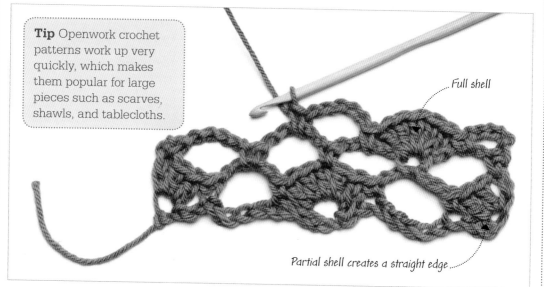

... Full shell

Partial shell creates a straight edge ....

3 Continue alternating shells and chain loops to complete the shell row. Work

mesh and shell rows alternately, working partial shells at ends on alternate shell rows.

Picot net stitch

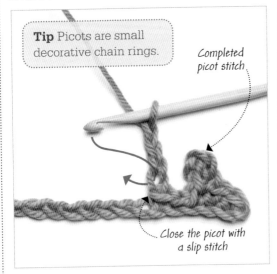

Tip Picots are small decorative chain rings.

Completed picot stitch

Close the picot with a slip stitch

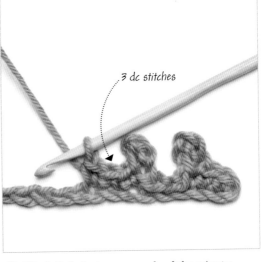

3 dc stitches

1 This pattern (see p.147) combines chain loops with chain rings called picots. Work 4 chains for each picot and close the ring with a slip stitch in the fourth chain from the hook.

2 Work 3 dc between each of the picots in each picot row as shown. The short stitches move the hook into position for the next picot without affecting the lacy pattern.

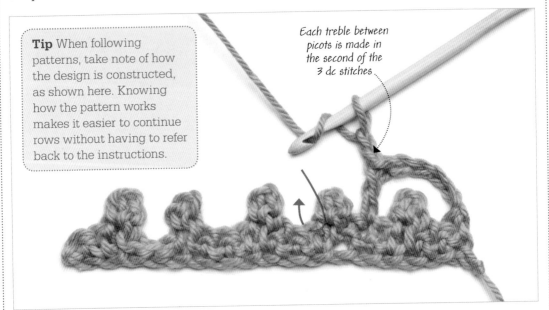

Tip When following patterns, take note of how the design is constructed, as shown here. Knowing how the pattern works makes it easier to continue rows without having to refer back to the instructions.

Each treble between picots is made in the second of the 3 dc stitches

3 After each picot row, work a 2-chain space above each picot and a tr between the picots as shown. Refer to the pattern on page 147 for full instructions.

Basic filet mesh

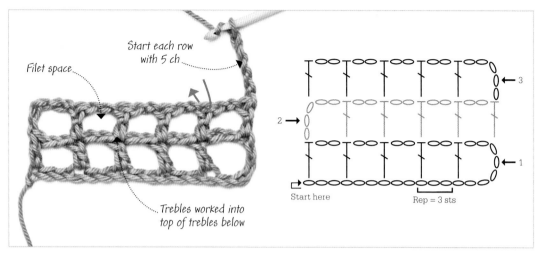

Start each row with 5 ch

Filet space

Trebles worked into top of trebles below

Start here

Rep = 3 sts

Filet crochet uses a square mesh structure to create patterns by filling in the squares. The diagram above explains how the basic filet mesh is worked with trebles and chains. Practise making a filet mesh before beginning a pattern. Start with a multiple of 3 ch (3 ch for each mesh square needed), plus 5 extra (to form the side edge and top of the first mesh square of the first row). The first tr goes in the eighth chain from the hook.

Filet blocks

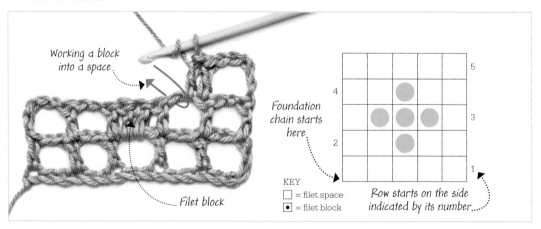

Working a block into a space

Foundation chain starts here

Filet block

KEY
□ = filet space
● = filet block

Row starts on the side indicated by its number

Filet crochet designs are made by filling in some of the mesh squares and leaving others empty. To make a filet block, instead of working 2 chains to form an empty square, work 2 trebles to fill in the square. An individual block consists of a treble on each side and 2 trebles in the centre. Use the chart above to make a cross motif, starting with 3 ch for each square plus 5 extra. Left-handed crocheters will need to work the chart in a mirror image.

Gallery of **Filet Stitch Patterns**

Filet lace makes lovely curtains, tablecloths, and edgings for pillowcases and towels. It looks best worked in a super-fine cotton yarn (see p.17). Follow the instructions on page 139 to work filet crochet from these charts. Repeat the charted motifs as many times as desired widthwise; to continue the pattern upwards, repeat from row 1 again.

Key

☐ = filet space

● = filet block

Diamonds Border

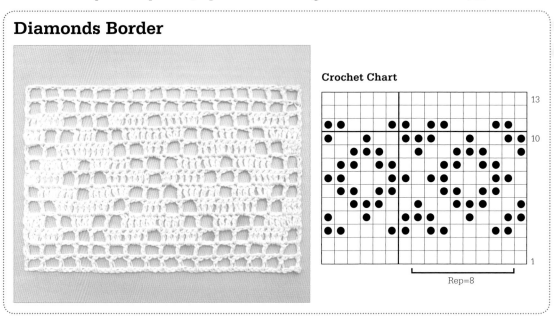

Crochet Chart

Rep=8

Crosses Border

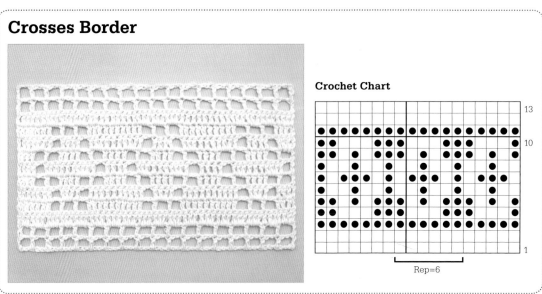

Crochet Chart

Rep=6

Heart

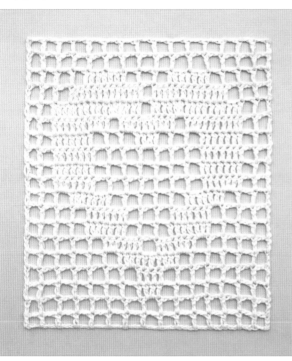

Crochet Chart

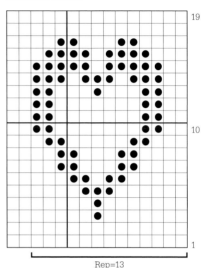

Rep=13

Bloom

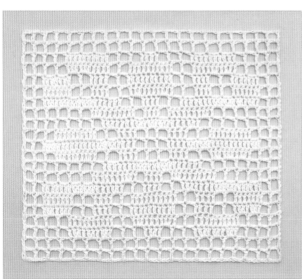

Crochet Chart

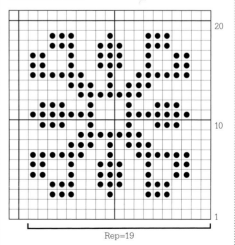

Rep=19

Make a String Bag

Do your part for the environment by making this
surprisingly roomy string bag. It holds more than a typical
plastic carrier bag and can be re-used over and over again.
The bag is made in the round, and has a solid bottom to
help prevent smaller objects from falling out.

Instructions

Yarn

You can use any DK cotton or cotton blend yarn. Here we have used Rowan Handknit Cotton 50g (85m/93yd)
352 Sea Foam x 2 balls

Hook Size

4.5mm hook

Size

38cm x 28cm (15in x 11in)

352 Sea Foam x 2

4.5mm hook

Pattern

Make 9 ch, ss in first ch to form a ring.

Round 1 3 ch, 11 tr in ring, ss in top of first 3-ch. (12sts)

Round 2 3 ch, 1 tr in same st, 2 tr in each st to end, ss in top of first 3-ch. (24sts)

Round 3 3 ch, 2 tr in next st, *1 tr in next st, 2 tr in next st; rep from * to end, ss in top of first 3-ch. (36sts)

Round 4 3 ch, 1 tr in next st, 2 tr in next st, *1 tr in each of next 2 sts, 2 tr in next st; rep from * to end, ss in top of first 3-ch. (48sts)

Round 5 3 ch, 1 tr in each of next 2 sts, 2 tr in next st, *1 tr in each of next 3 sts, 2 tr in next st; rep from * to end, ss in top of first 3-ch. (60sts)

Round 6 3 ch, 1 tr in each of next 3 sts, 2 tr in next st, *1 tr in each of next 4 sts, 2 tr in next st; rep from * to end, ss in top of first 3-ch. (72sts)

Round 7 3 ch, 1 tr in each of next 4 sts, 2 tr in next st, *1 tr in each of next 5 sts, 2 tr in next st; rep from * to end, ss in top of first 3-ch. (84sts)

Round 8 *4 ch, miss 2 sts, 1 dc in next st; rep from * to end, omit last dc, end with a ss at base of first 4-ch. (28 4-ch loops)

Round 9 Ss in each of next 2 ch, *4 ch, 1 dc in next 4-ch loop; rep from * to end, ending with a ss in first ss at beg of round.

Rounds 10–14 Rep round 9.

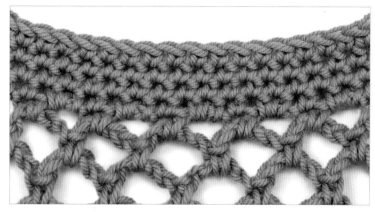

Round 15 Ss in each of next 2 ch, *6 ch, 1 dc in next 4-ch loop; rep from * to end, ending with a ss in first ss at beg of round.

Round 16 Ss in each of next 3 ch, *6 ch, 1 dc in next 6-ch loop; rep from * to end, ending with a ss in first ss at beg of round.

Rounds 17–21 Rep round 16.

Top of the bag

Rounds of double crochet stitches across the top of the bag give it structure and prevent it from stretching too much when carried.

Round 22 Ss in each of next 3 ch, *4 ch, 1 dc in next 6-ch loop; rep from * to end, ending with a ss in first ss at beg of round.
Rounds 23–27 Rep round 9.
Round 28 *2 ch, 1 dc in next 4-ch loop; rep from * to end, ss at base of first 2-ch loop.

Top
Round 29 1 ch, *2 dc in next 2-ch loop, 1 dc in next dc; rep from* to end, ss in first 1-ch to join. (82sts)

Create handles
Round 30 1 ch, 1 dc in each of next 8 sts, 24 ch (handle can be lengthened by adding more ch, as desired), miss 23 sts, 1 dc in 24th st and in each of next 17 sts, 24 ch (handle can be lengthened by adding more ch, as desired), miss 23 sts, 1 dc in 24th st and in each of rem 10 sts, ss in first st to join.
Round 31 1 ch, 1 dc in same st and in each st to handle, 1 dc in each ch across handle, 1 dc in each st to next handle, 1 dc in each ch across handle, 1 dc in each st to end of round, ss in first st to join.
Round 32 1 ch, 1 dc in same st and in each st all around bag, ss in first st to join.
Fasten off, weave in ends.

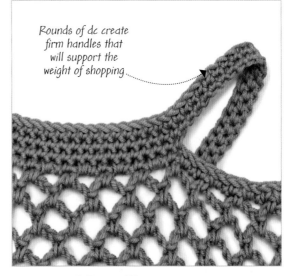

Rounds of dc create firm handles that will support the weight of shopping....

Integral handles

Handles are created by working chain stitches within the four rounds of double crochet that form the top border of the bag.

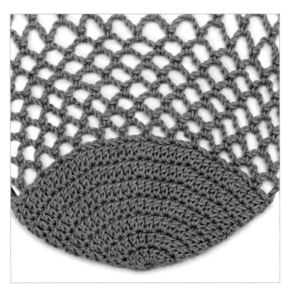

Solid base

A closed bottom and smaller chain loops in the lower half of the bag help to ensure that smaller items won't fall out easily.

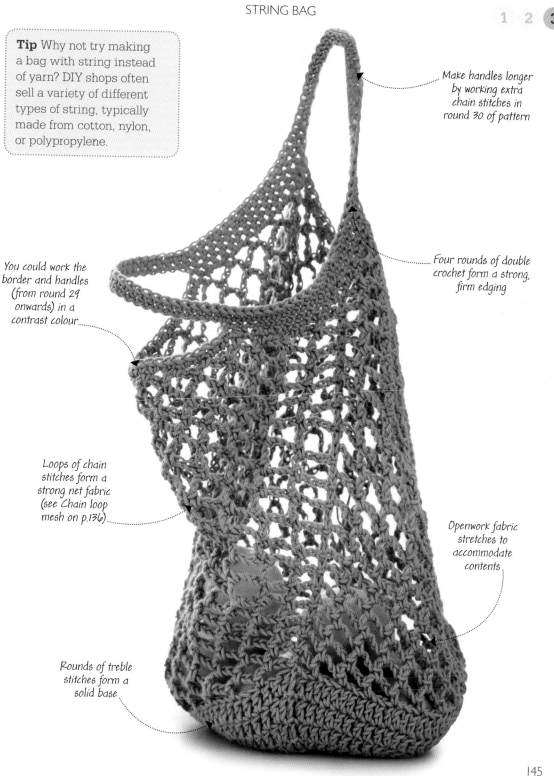

Tip Why not try making a bag with string instead of yarn? DIY shops often sell a variety of different types of string, typically made from cotton, nylon, or polypropylene.

Make handles longer by working extra chain stitches in round 30 of pattern

Four rounds of double crochet form a strong, firm edging

You could work the border and handles (from round 29 onwards) in a contrast colour

Loops of chain stitches form a strong net fabric (see Chain loop mesh on p.136)

Openwork fabric stretches to accommodate contents

Rounds of treble stitches form a solid base

Gallery of **Openwork Stitch Patterns**

Openwork crochet stitches are popular because of their lacy appearance and because they are quicker to work than solid crochet textures. They also drape gracefully due to their airy construction. Any of these easy stitch patterns would make an attractive shawl or scarf. A glance at the symbol diagram will reveal which basic stitches and simple stitch techniques are involved.

Chain Loop Mesh

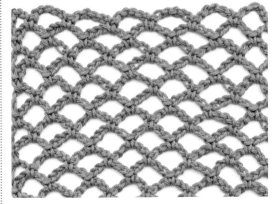

Make a multiple of 4 ch, plus 2 extra.
Row 1 1 dc in 6th ch from hook, *5 ch, miss next 3 ch, 1 dc in next ch; rep from * to end, turn.

Row 2 *5 ch, 1 dc in next 5-ch loop; rep from * to end, turn.
Rep row 2 to form patt.

Arched Mesh Stitch

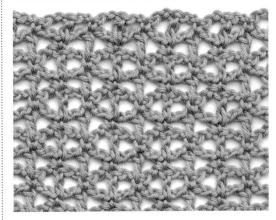

Make a multiple of 4 ch.
Row 1 1 dc in 2nd ch from hook, 2 ch, miss next ch, 1 tr in next ch, *2 ch, miss next ch, 1 dc in next ch, 2 ch, miss next ch, 1 tr in next ch; rep from * to end, turn.

Row 2 1 ch (does not count as a st), 1 dc in first tr, 2 ch, 1 tr in next dc, *2 ch, 1 dc in next tr, 2 ch, 1 tr in next dc; rep from * to end, turn.
Rep row 2 to form patt.

Open Shell Stitch

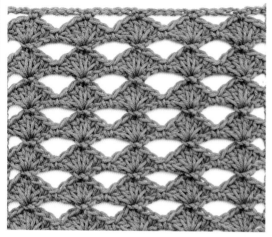

Make a multiple of 6 ch, plus 2 extra.
Row 1 (RS) 1 dc in 2nd ch from hook, *miss next 2 ch, 5 tr in next ch, miss next 2 ch, 1 dc in next ch; rep from * to end, turn.
Row 2 5 ch (counts as first tr and 2-ch sp), 1 dc in centre tr of first shell, *5 ch, 1 dc in centre tr of next

shell; rep from *, ending with 2 ch, 1 tr in last dc, turn.
Row 3 1 ch (does not count as a st), 1 dc in first tr, *5 tr in next dc, 1 dc in next 5-ch loop; rep from *, working last dc of last rep in 3rd ch from last dc, turn.
Rep rows 2 and 3 to form patt.

Picot Net Stitch

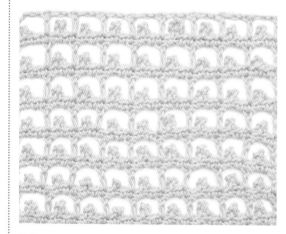

Make a multiple of 3 ch, plus 2 extra.
Row 1 (RS) 1 dc in 2nd ch from hook, 1 dc in next ch, *4 ch, 1 ss in 4th ch from hook (called 1 picot), 1 dc in each of next 3 ch; rep from * omitting 1 dc at end of last rep, turn.
Row 2 5 ch (counts as 1 tr and 2-ch sp), miss first 3 dc (which includes 2 dc before picot and 1 dc after

picot), 1 tr in next dc, *2 ch, miss next 2 dc (which includes 1 dc on each side of picot), 1 tr in next dc; rep from * to end, turn.
Row 3 1 ch (does not count as a st), 1 dc in first tr,*(1 dc, 1 picot, 1 dc) in next 2-ch sp, 1 dc in next tr; rep from *, working last dc of last rep in 3rd ch from last tr, turn.
Rep rows 2 and 3 to form patt.

Shell Mesh Stitch

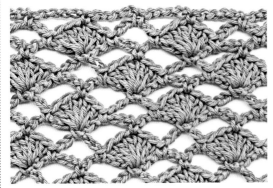

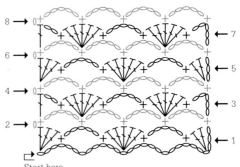

Start here

Make a multiple of 12 ch, plus 4 extra.

Row 1 (RS) 2 tr in 4th ch from hook, *miss next 2 ch, 1 dc in next ch, 5 ch, miss next 5 ch, 1 dc in next ch, miss next 2 ch, 5 tr in next ch; rep from *, ending last rep with 3 tr (instead of 5 tr) in last ch, turn.

Row 2 1 ch (does not count as a st), 1 dc in first tr, *5 ch, 1 dc in next 5-ch loop, 5 ch, 1 dc in 3rd tr of next 5-tr shell; rep from *, working last dc of last rep in top of 3-ch at end, turn.

Row 3 *5 ch, 1 dc in next 5-ch loop, 5 tr in next dc, 1 dc in next 5-ch loop; rep from *, ending with 2 ch, 1 tr in last dc, turn.

Row 4 1 ch (does not count as a st), 1 dc in first tr, *5 ch, 1 dc in 3rd tr of next 5-tr shell, 5 ch, 1 dc in next 5-ch loop; rep from * to end, turn.

Row 5 3 ch (counts as first tr), 2 tr in first dc, *1 dc in next 5-ch loop, 5 ch, 1 dc in next 5-ch loop, 5 tr in next dc; rep from *, ending last rep with 3 tr (instead of 5 tr) in last dc, turn.

Rep rows 2–5 to form patt.

Blocks Lace

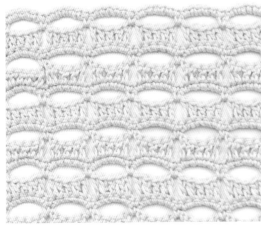

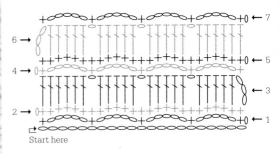

Start here

Make a multiple of 5 ch, plus 2 extra.

Row 1 (RS) 1 dc in 2nd ch from hook, *5 ch, miss next 4 ch, 1 dc in next ch; rep from * to end, turn.

Row 2 1 ch (does not count as a st), 1 dc in first dc, *5 dc in next 5-ch loop, 1 dc in next dc; rep from * to end, turn.

Row 3 3 ch (counts as first tr), miss first dc, 1 tr in each of next 5 dc, *1 ch, miss next dc, 1 tr in each of next 5 dc; rep from * to last dc, 1 tr in last dc, turn.

Row 4 1 ch (does not count as a st), 1 dc in first tr, *5 ch, 1 dc in next 1-ch sp; rep from *, working last dc of last rep in top of 3-ch at end, turn.

Rep rows 2–4 to form patt.

Tiara Lace

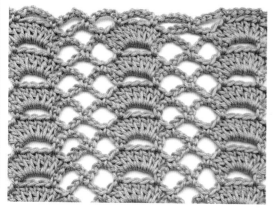

Make a multiple of 12 ch.
Row 1 (WS) 1 dc in 2nd ch from hook, *5 ch, miss next 3 ch, 1 dc in next ch; rep from * to last 2 ch, 2 ch, miss next ch, 1 tr in last ch, turn.
Row 2 (RS) 1 ch (does not count as a st), 1 dc in first st, miss next 2-ch sp, 7 tr in next 5-ch loop, 1 dc in next 5-ch loop, *5 ch, 1 dc in next 5-ch loop, 7 tr in next 5-ch loop, 1 dc in next 5-ch loop; rep from *, ending with 2 ch,

1 dtr in last dc, turn.
Row 3 1 ch (does not count as a st), 1 dc in first dtr, 5 ch, 1 dc in 2nd tr of next 7-tr shell, 5 ch, 1 dc in 6th tr of same shell, *5 ch, 1 dc in next 5-ch loop, 5 ch, 1 dc in 2nd tr of next 7-tr shell, 5 ch, 1 dc in 6th tr of same shell; rep from *, ending with 2 ch, 1 dtr in last dc, turn.
Rep rows 2 and 3 to form patt.

Fans Stitch

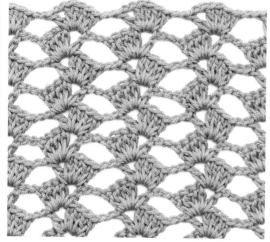

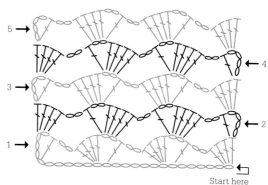

Make a multiple of 7 ch, plus 4 extra.
Row 1 1 tr in 5th ch from hook, 2 ch, miss next 5 ch, 4 tr in next ch, *2 ch, 1 tr in next ch, 2 ch, miss next 5 ch, 4 tr in next ch; rep from * to end, turn.
Row 2 4 ch, 1 tr in first tr, *2 ch, miss next 2-ch sp, (4 tr,

2 ch, 1 tr) in following 2-ch sp; rep from * to last 2-ch sp, miss last 2-ch sp and work 4 tr in 4-ch loop at end, turn.
Rep row 2 to form patt.

Make a Lacy Scarf

This lacy, openwork scarf is made using the fans stitch
from page 149. The lacy effect is created using alternating
chain loops and clusters of treble crochet stitches, making
it simple enough for a first attempt at openwork.

Instructions

Yarn
You can use any DK yarn. Here we have used Sirdar Country Style DK 100g (155m/169yd)
600 Dewberry x 1 ball

Hook Size
4mm hook

Size
18cm x 180cm (7in x 71in) or desired length

600 Dewberry x 1

4mm hook

Pattern
Work 33 ch.

Row 1 1 tr in 5th ch from hook, *2 ch, miss 5 ch, 3 tr in next ch, 2 ch, tr in next ch; rep from * 3 times more.

Row 2 4 ch, turn, 1 tr in first 2-ch sp, *2 ch, (4 tr, 2 ch, 1 tr) in next 2-ch sp; rep from * twice more, 2 ch, 3 tr in last sp, 1 tr in 3rd ch of 4-ch in row below.

Rep row 2 until piece measures 180cm (71in) or desired length. Fasten off, weave in ends.

Edging
This pattern forms a neat edge on the two long sides of the scarf, and a slightly scalloped effect at the ends.

Pattern
The simple, single-row repeat forms a pattern of asymmetrical stitches and spaces.

How to **Crochet Colour Patterns**

Patterns that change colour in the middle of a row require either the jacquard or the intarsia method. Jacquard carries the colour not in use across the whole row, whereas intarsia drops and picks up colours as you work along the row. Both are usually worked in double crochet.

Jacquard method

JACQUARD CHART

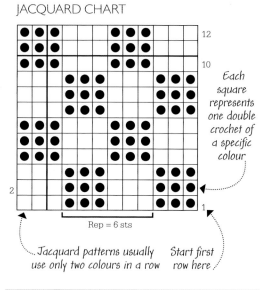

12

10

Each square represents one double crochet of a specific colour

2

Rep = 6 sts

1

...Jacquard patterns usually use only two colours in a row

Start first row here

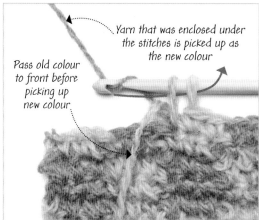

Yarn that was enclosed under the stitches is picked up as the new colour

Pass old colour to front before picking up new colour

Enclose the not-in-use colour inside stitches

1 Work up to the last yrh of the stitch before the colour change, then pass the old colour to the front, over the top of the new colour. Use the new colour to complete the dc.

2 Position the old colour along the top of the row below. Work the stitches in the new colour over the old yarn to trap it within the stitches until it is needed again.

Intarsia method

INTARSIA CHART

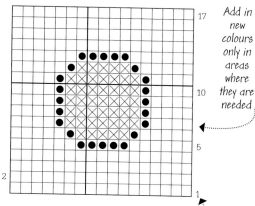

17

10

5

2

1

Add in new colours only in areas where they are needed

Start first row here and read rows back and forth as for a stitch diagram

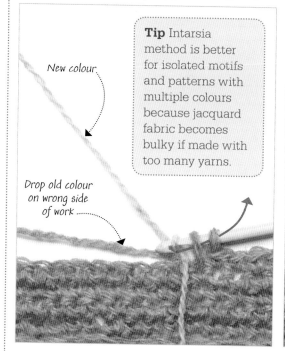

New colour

Tip Intarsia method is better for isolated motifs and patterns with multiple colours because jacquard fabric becomes bulky if made with too many yarns.

Drop old colour on wrong side of work

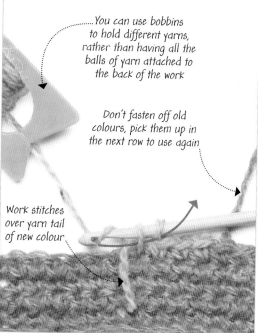

...You can use bobbins to hold different yarns, rather than having all the balls of yarn attached to the back of the work

Don't fasten off old colours, pick them up in the next row to use again

Work stitches over yarn tail of new colour

1 Work to the position on the chart where the motif begins, but stop before working the last yrh of the previous stitch. Then complete the dc using the new colour.

2 Work dc in the new colour as shown. Then join in another ball (or length of yarn) for the next area of background colour. Use a separate ball of yarn for each area of colour.

153

Make a Tote Bag

Practise colourwork techniques with this attractive bag.
The zigzag border is worked using the jacquard technique
and the patch pocket with a pear motif is an example of an
intarsia pattern. You will need to work from a chart, which
is a lot easier than you might think.

Instructions

Yarn

You can use any DK weight cotton or cotton blend yarn. Here we have used Debbie Bliss Cotton DK 50g (84m/91yd) in 4 colours

A: 13067 Lilac x 5 balls
B: 13002 Ecru x 1 ball
C: 13068 Cloud x 1 ball
D: 13063 Gold x 1 ball

13067 Lilac x 5

13002 Ecru x 1

13068 Cloud x 1

13063 Gold x 1

4mm hook

Hook Size

4mm hook

Notions

Yarn bobbins

Tension

16 dc and 20 rows to 10cm (4in)

Size

32cm x 25cm (12½in x 9¾in); to fit A4 size documents

Pattern
Bag (make 2, for front and back)

With yarn A, make 42 ch.

Row 1 (RS) 1 dc in 2nd ch from hook, 1 dc in each ch to end. (41 sts)

Row 2 1 ch (does not count as a st), 1 dc in each dc of previous row. Rep row 2 56 times.

Row 59 1 ch, 1 dc in each of first 3 dc, 1 dc in next dc, joining in yarn B on last yrh of st, then follow chart below, using the jacquard method, for rem 5 rows.
Cut yarn, leaving a tail, and fasten off.

Handle (make 2)
With yarn A, make 6 ch.
Row 1 (RS) 1 dc in 2nd ch from hook, 1 dc in each ch to end. (5 sts)
Row 2 1 ch (does not count as a

st), 1 dc in each dc of previous row. Rep row 2 95 times.
Cut yarn, leaving a tail, and fasten off.

Pocket See p.156 for instructions.

Finishing
Stitch side seams and base of bag using a blunt-ended yarn needle and matching yarn. Pin pocket to centre front of bag and sew edges using overcast stitch (see p.47), leaving top edge open. Stitch ends of handles to top edge of bag.

Jacquard chart

In this chart, the black dots denote the lilac yarn and the white spaces denote the ecru coloured yarn.

Key ● = yarn A   □ = yarn B

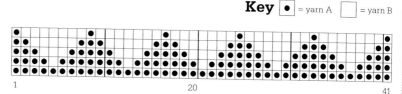

1   20   41

Zigzag border

The border of the bag is worked using the jacquard method. Because the trailing yarns are hidden within the stitches, jacquard patterns are reversible and look good on both sides.

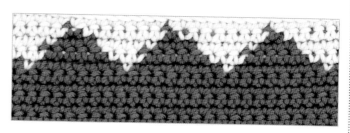

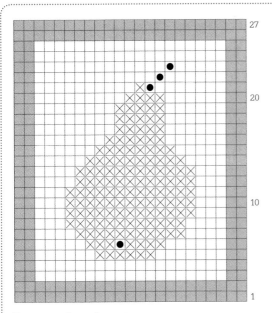

Key   ● = yarn A   □ = yarn B
          ▨ = yarn C   ⊠ = yarn D

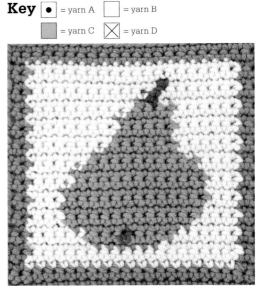

Intarsia chart

Follow the colour key above to work one double crochet stitch for every square.

Intarsia patch

The yarn strands are carried across the back of the work to keep the front neat.

Pocket (make 1)

With yarn C, make 24 ch.
Row 1 (RS) 1 dc in 2nd ch from hook, 1 dc in each ch to end. (23 sts)
Beg working from chart, using the intarsia method, starting from row 2 (WS).
Cut yarn, leaving a tail, and fasten off.

Bobbins of yarn

Yarn bobbins (see p.15) can be used to keep colours not in use out of the way, or alternatively wind lengths of yarn into small balls that can be unravelled as you work.

Handles are narrow strips crocheted separately and stitched in place......

Double crochet makes a firm, dense texture, ideal for hardwearing items....

Back of work

Dropping colours in intarsia

A colour not currently in use is held at the back of the work on a yarn bobbin. When it is needed again, simply bring it to the front, drop the current yarn at the back and continue working.

Side seams and base of bag are stitched together (see p.46)

Ensure that you place the pocket centrally on the front of the bag

Tip Finished colour motifs always look shorter than a chart depicts because double crochet stitches are not square. They are shorter than they are wide.

Gallery of **Colourwork Stitch Patterns**

Working stitch patterns and textures in stripes is easy to do and looks impressive. Re-familiarise yourself with techniques of switching and carrying yarn on page 39, and have fun choosing colours (see p.20). In the diagrams, the symbol tones denote row changes and not colour changes, so use colours as explained in the written instructions.

Simple Zigzag Stitch

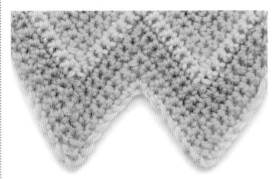

Note: When working from diagram, rep rows 2 and 3 for stitch pattern (since colour changes are not indicated on diagrams).

This pattern is worked in 3 colours (A, B, C).
With yarn C, make a multiple of 16 ch, plus 2 extra.
Row 1 (RS) With yarn A, 2 dc in 2nd ch from hook, *1 dc in each of next 7 ch, miss next ch, 1 dc in each of next 7 ch, 3 dc in next ch; rep from * to end, working 2 dc (instead of 3 dc) in last ch, turn.
Row 2 With yarn A, 1 ch (does not count as a st), 2 dc in first dc, *1 dc in each of next 7 dc, miss next 2 dc, 1 dc in each of next 7 dc, 3 dc in next dc; rep from * to end, working 2 dc (instead of 3 dc) in last dc, turn.
Rows 3 and 4 With yarn B, rep row 2 twice.
Rows 5 and 6 With yarn C, rep row 2 twice.
Rows 7 and 8 With yarn A, rep row 2 twice.
Rep rows 3–8 to form patt.

Coloured Tweed Stitch

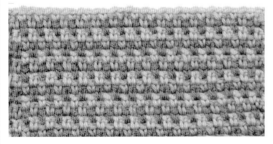

This pattern is worked in 3 colours (A, B, C).
With yarn A, make a multiple of 2 ch.
Row 1 With yarn A, 1 dc in 2nd ch from hook, *1 ch, miss next ch, 1 dc in next ch; rep from * to end, turn.
Row 2 With yarn B, 1 ch (does not count as a st), 1 dc in first dc, 1 dc in next 1-ch sp, *1 ch, 1 dc in next 1-ch sp; rep from * to last dc, 1 dc in last dc, turn.
Row 3 With yarn C, 1 ch (does not count as a st), 1 dc in first dc, *1 ch, 1 dc in next 1-ch sp; rep from * to last 2 dc, 1 ch, miss next dc, 1 dc in last dc, turn.
Row 4 With yarn A, rep row 2.
Row 5 With yarn B, rep row 3.
Row 6 With yarn C, rep row 2.
Row 7 With yarn A, rep row 3.
Rep rows 2–7 to form patt.

Spike Stitch Stripes

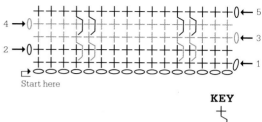

Start here

KEY

spike stitch

NOTE: spike st = do not work into next st but instead insert hook from front to back through top of st one row below this st, yrh and draw a loop through, lengthening the loop to the height of the row being worked (and enclosing the missed st), yrh and draw through both loops on hook to complete an elongated dc.
This pattern is worked in 2 colours (A, B).
With yarn A, make a multiple of 8 ch, plus 1 extra.
Row 1 (RS) With yarn A, 1 dc in 2nd ch from hook, 1 dc in each of rem ch, turn.

Row 2 With yarn A, 1 ch (does not count as a st), 1 dc in each dc to end, turn.
Row 3 With yarn B, 1 ch (does not count as a st), *1 dc in each of next 3 dc, (1 spike st in top of st one row below next st) twice, 1 dc in each of next 3 dc; rep from * to end, turn.
Row 4 With yarn B, rep row 2.
Row 5 With yarn A, rep row 3.
Rep rows 2–5 to form patt.

Bobble Stripe

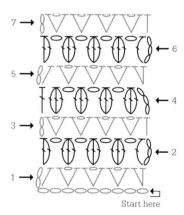

Start here

NOTE: bobble = 3-tr bobble (see p.118).
This pattern is worked in 3 colours (A, B, C).
With yarn A, make a multiple of 2 ch, plus 1 extra.
Work the following rows in stripes, repeating this stripe sequence – 1 row A, 1 row B, 1 row C.
Row 1 (WS) 1 htr in 3rd ch from hook, *miss next ch, (1 htr, 1 ch, 1 htr) in next ch; rep from * to last 2 ch, miss next ch, 2 htr in last ch, turn.
Row 2 (RS) 3 ch (counts as first tr), 1 tr in first htr, *1 ch, 1 bobble in next 1-ch sp; rep from *, ending with 1 ch, at end of row; work a 2-tr bobble in top of 2-ch, turn.

Row 3 2 ch (counts as first htr), *(1 htr, 1 ch, 1 htr) in next 1-ch sp; rep from *, ending with 1 htr in top of 3-ch, turn.
Row 4 3 ch (counts as first tr), 1 bobble in next 1-ch sp, *1 ch, 1 bobble in next 1-ch sp; rep from *, ending with 1 tr in top of 2-ch at end, turn.
Row 5 2 ch (counts as first htr), 1 htr in first tr, *(1 htr, 1 ch, 1 htr) in next 1-ch sp; rep from *, ending with 2 htr in top of 3-ch at end, turn.
Rep rows 2–5 to form patt, while continuing stripe sequence.

How to **Crochet Motifs**

Small shapes and blocks of crochet can be used as decorations or
combined to make beautiful blankets or cushion covers. Use these
techniques to make weaving in tails and joining blocks easier.

Joining in a new colour

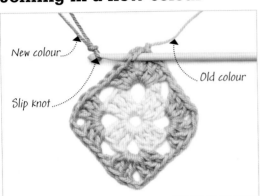

New colour

Slip knot

Old colour

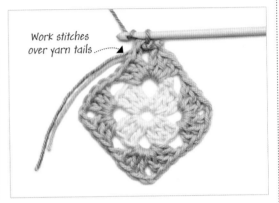

Work stitches
over yarn tails

1 Join in the new colour with a slip stitch to
make a firm attachment. Make a slip knot
with the new colour and remove it from the
hook. Then insert the hook at the new position
and draw the slip knot through.

2 Start the new round with the specified
number of chains, drawing the first chain
through the slip knot. Work the next stitches
over the yarn tails so that there are fewer ends
to weave in later.

Joining motifs

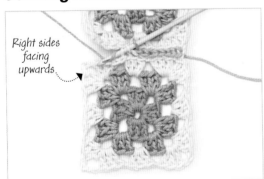

Right sides
facing
upwards

Right sides
together
means ridge
will be
hidden on
wrong side

FLAT SLIP-STITCH SEAM
For a slip-stitch seam that gives a streamlined
finish, lay the two motifs side by side and
work slip stitches through only the back loop
of the top of a stitch on each motif.

DOUBLE-CROCHET SEAM
A double crochet seam forms a ridge, which
you can hide or make into a feature. Hold the
two motifs together and work through only
the back loops of the stitches on each motif.

Gallery of **Motif Patterns**

Motifs are great for using up yarn scraps and can be used as lovely embellishments or stitched together to make bags and throws, for example. All the shapes in this gallery are made in the round.

Granny Square

Note: In this version of the granny square pattern, the rounds start and finish at same position (at the last treble of each round), making it easy to work continuous rounds. This square is worked in 4 colours (A, B, C, D), using a different colour for each round.

With yarn A, make 4 ch and join with a ss to first ch to form a ring.

Round 1 (RS) With yarn A, 5 ch (counts as 1 tr and 2-ch sp), (3 tr in ring, 2 ch [these 2-ch form a corner sp]) 3 times, 2 tr in ring, join with a ss to 3rd of 5-ch. Fasten off yarn A.

Round 2 With yarn B, join with a ss to any 2-ch corner sp, 5 ch, 3 tr in same corner sp, *1 ch, (3 tr, 2 ch, 3 tr) in next 2-ch corner sp; rep from* twice more, 1 ch, 2 tr in same corner sp as 5-ch at beg of round, join with a ss to 3rd of 5-ch. Fasten off yarn B.

Round 3 With yarn C, join to any 2-ch corner sp, 5 ch, 3 tr in same corner sp, *1 ch, 3 tr in next 1-ch sp, 1 ch, (3 tr, 2 ch, 3 tr) in next 2-ch corner sp; rep from * twice more, 1 ch, 3 tr in next 1-ch sp, 1 ch, 2 tr in same sp as 5-ch at beg of round, join with a ss to 3rd of 5-ch. Fasten off yarn C.

Round 4 With yarn D, join to any 2-ch corner sp, 5 ch, 3 tr in same corner sp, *(1 ch, 3 tr in next 1-ch sp) twice, 1 ch, (3 tr, 2 ch, 3 tr) in next 2-ch corner sp; rep from * twice more, (1 ch, 3 tr in next 1-ch sp) twice, 1 ch, 2 tr in same sp as 5-ch at beg of round, join with a ss to 3rd of 5-ch. Fasten off.

Plain Square

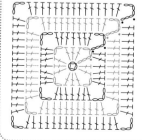

This square is worked in 3 colours (A, B, C).

With yarn A, make 4 ch and join with a ss to first ch to form a ring.

Round 1 (RS) 5 ch (counts as 1 tr and 2-ch sp), (3 tr in ring, 2 ch) 3 times, 2 tr in ring, join with a ss to 3rd of 5-ch.

Round 2 1 ss in next ch, 7 ch (counts as 1 tr and 4-ch sp), 2 tr in same 2-ch corner sp, *1 tr in each of next 3 tr, (2 tr, 4 ch, 2 tr) in next 2-ch corner sp; rep from * twice more, 1 tr in each of next 3 sts (working last of these tr in top of turning ch at beg of previous round), 1 tr in same sp as 7-ch at beg of round, join with a ss to 3rd of 7-ch. Fasten off yarn A.

Round 3 With yarn B, join to any 4-ch corner sp, 7 ch, 2 tr in same corner sp, *1 tr in each tr along this side of square, (2 tr, 4 ch, 2 tr) in next 4-ch corner sp; rep from * twice more, 1 tr in each tr along this side of square (working last of turning ch at beg of previous round), 1 tr in same sp as 7-ch at beg of round, join with a ss to 3rd of 7-ch. Fasten off yarn B.

Round 4 With yarn C, rep round 3. Fasten off.

Flower Hexagon

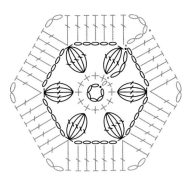

Note: bobble = (yrh and insert hook in dc, yrh and draw a loop through, yrh and draw through first 2 loops on hook) 5 times all in same dc (6 loops now on hook), yrh and draw through all 6 loops on hook. This hexagon is worked in 2 colours (A, B).

With yarn A, make 6 ch and join with a ss to first ch to form a ring.

Round 1 (RS) 1 ch, 12 dc in ring, join with a ss to first dc.

Round 2 3 ch, (yrh and insert hook in same dc as last ss, yrh and draw a loop through, yrh and draw through first 2 loops on hook) 4 times in same dc (5 loops now on hook), yrh and draw through all 5 loops on hook (counts as first bobble), *5 ch, miss next dc, 1 bobble in next dc; rep from * 4 times more, 5 ch, join with a ss to top of first bobble. Fasten off yarn A.

Round 3 With yarn B, join with a ss to top of any bobble, 5 ch (counts as 1 tr and 2-ch sp), 1 tr in same place as ss, *5 tr in next 5-ch sp, (1 tr, 2 ch, 1 tr) in top of next bobble; rep from * 4 times more, 5 tr in next 5-ch sp, join with a ss to 3rd of 5-ch at beg of round. Fasten off.

Simple Hexagon

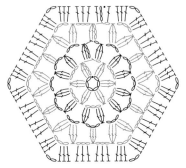

Note: cluster (cl) = (yrh and insert hook in sp, yrh and draw a loop through, yrh and draw through first 2 loops on hook) 3 times all in same sp (4 loops now on hook), yrh and draw through all 4 loops on hook.

This hexagon is worked in 3 colours (A, B, C).

With yarn A, make 6 ch and join with a ss to first ch to form a ring.

Round 1 (RS) 3 ch, tr2tog (counts as first cl), (3 ch, 1 cl in ring) 5 times, 1 ch, join with 1 htr in top of first cl.

Round 2 3 ch, tr2tog in sp formed by 1-htr, *3 ch, (1 cl, 3 ch, 1 cl) in next 3-ch sp; rep from * 4 times more, 3 ch, 1 cl in next 1-ch sp, 1 ch, join with 1 htr in top of first cl,

changing to yarn B with last yrh of htr. Cut yarn A.

Round 3 With yarn B, 3 ch, tr2tog in sp formed by 1-htr (counts as first cl), *3 ch, (1 cl, 3 ch, 1 cl) in next 3-ch sp, 3 ch, 1 cl in next 3-ch sp; rep from * 4 times more, 3 ch, (1 cl, 3 ch, 1 cl) in next 3-ch sp, 1 ch, join with 1 htr in top of first cl changing to yarn C with last yrh of htr. Cut yarn B.

Round 4 With yarn C, 3 ch, 1 tr in sp formed by 1-htr, *3 tr in next 3-ch sp, (3 tr, 2 ch, 3 tr) in next 3-ch sp, 3 ch, 1 tr in next 3-ch sp; rep from * 4 times more, 3 tr in next 3-ch sp, (3 tr, 2 ch, 3 tr) in next 3-ch sp, 1 tr in next 1-ch sp, join with a ss to 3rd of 3-ch at beg of round. Fasten off.

Button Flower

Note: cluster (cl) = (yrh twice and insert hook in sp, yrh and draw a loop through, [yrh and draw through first 2 loops on hook] twice) 4 times all in same sp (5 loops now on hook), yrh and draw through all 5 loops now on hook.
This flower is worked in 2 colours (A, B).
With yarn A, make 4 ch and join with a ss to first ch to form a ring.
Round 1 (RS) 4 ch (counts as first dtr), 20 dtr in ring, join with a ss to 4th of 4-ch. Fasten off yarn A.

Round 2 With yarn B, join with a ss to same place as last ss, 1 ch (does not count as a st), 1 dc in same place as last ss, (5 ch, miss next 2 dtr, 1 dc in next dtr) 6 times, 5 ch, join with a ss to first dc of round.
Round 3 * (1 ss, 4 ch, 1 cluster, 4 ch, 1 ss) in next 5-ch loop; rep from * 6 times more, join with a ss to same place as last ss in round 2.
Fasten off.
Sew a small button on to the centre of the flower.

Short Loop Flower

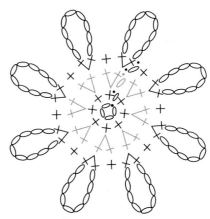

This flower is worked in 2 colours (A, B).
With yarn A, make 4 ch and join with a ss to first ch to form a ring.
Round 1 (RS) 1 ch (does not count as a st), 8 dc in ring, join with a ss to first dc of round.
Round 2 1 ch (does not count as a st), 2 dc in same place as ss, *2 dc in next dc; rep from * to end, join with a ss to first dc of round. (16sts)

Fasten off yarn A.
Round 3 With yarn B, join with a ss to any dc, 1 ch, (1 dc, 9 ch, 1 dc) in same place as last ss, 1 dc in next dc, * (1 dc, 9 ch, 1 dc) in next dc, 1 dc in next dc; rep from * 6 times more, join with a ss to first dc of round.
Fasten off.

Long Loop Flower

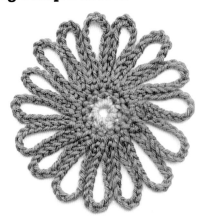
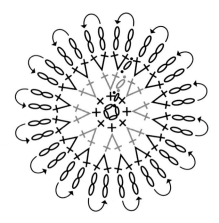

This flower is worked in 3 colours (A, B, C).
With yarn A, make 4 ch and join with a ss to first ch to form a ring.
Round 1 (RS) 1 ch (does not count as a st), 8 dc in ring, join with a ss to first dc of round. Fasten off yarn A.
Round 2 With yarn B, join with a ss to any dc, 1 ch (does not count as a st), 2 dc in same place as last ss, *2 dc in next dc; rep from * to end, join with a ss to first dc of round. Fasten off yarn B. (16sts)
Round 3 With yarn C, join with a ss to any dc, 1 ch, (1 dc, 17 ch, 1 dc) all in same place as last ss, * (1 dc, 17 ch, 1 dc) in next dc; rep from * 14 times more, join with a ss to first dc of round.
Fasten off.

Pentagon Flower

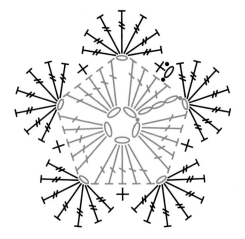

This flower is worked in 2 colours (A, B).
With yarn A, make 5 ch and join with a ss to first ch to form a ring.
Round 1 (RS) 3 ch (counts as first tr), 4 tr in ring, (1 ch, 5 tr in ring) 4 times, 1 ch, join with a ss to top of 3-ch at beg of round. Fasten off yarn A.

Round 2 With yarn B, join with a ss to a centre tr of any 5-tr group, 1 ch, 1 dc in same place as last ss, (7 dtr in next 1-ch sp, 1 dc in centre tr of next 5-tr group) 4 times, 7 dtr in next 1-ch sp, join with a ss to first dc of round.
Fasten off.

Square Petal Flower

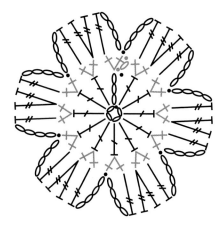

This flower is worked in 3 colours (A, B, C).

With yarn A, make 4 ch and join with a ss to first ch to form a ring.

Round 1 (RS) 3 ch (counts as first tr), 11 tr in ring, join with a ss to top of 3-ch at beg of round. Fasten off yarn A.

Round 2 With B, join with a ss same place as last ss, 1 ch (does not count as a st), 2 dc in same place as last ss, 2 dc in each tr to end, join with a ss to first dc of round. Fasten off yarn B. (24 sts)

Round 3 With yarn C, join with a ss to any dc, *4 ch, 1 dtr in next dc, 2 dtr in next dc, 1 dtr in next dc, 4 ch, 1 ss in next dc; rep from * 5 times more, working last ss in same place as first ss of round.

Fasten off.

Simple Leaf

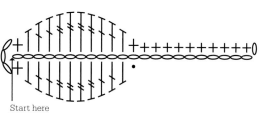

Start here

Note: The leaf is worked in one row, around both sides of the foundation chain.

To begin leaf and stem, make 23 ch.

Row 1 (RS) Working into only one loop of each foundation chain, work 1 dc in 2nd ch from hook, 1 dc in each of next 10 ch (this completes the stem), 1 htr in next ch, 1 tr in each of next 2 ch, 1 dtr in each of next 4 ch, 1 tr in each of next 2 ch, 1 htr in next ch, 1 dc in last ch, 3 ch, then continue working along other side of foundation ch (working into rem loop of each ch) as follows: 1 dc in first ch, 1 htr in next ch, 1 tr in each of next 2 ch, 1 dtr in each of next 4 ch, 1 tr in each of next 2 ch, 1 htr in next ch, 1 ss in next ch.

Fasten off.

Press stem flat.

Make a Patchwork Blanket

This beautiful blanket is made by joining individual squares – a variation of the plain square on page 161 – then adding a treble crochet border. You can make this blanket any size you wish, by using more or fewer squares.

Instructions

Yarn

You can use any DK yarn. Here we have used Stylecraft Special DK 100g (295m/322yd) in 3 colours

A: 1005 Cream x 3 balls

B: 1241 Fondant x 2 balls

C: 1432 Wisteria x 2 balls

1005 Cream x 3

1241 Fondant x 2

1432 Wisteria x 2

Hook Size

4mm hook

4mm hook

Size

110cm x 94cm (43in x 37in)

Pattern

Square

With yarn A, make 4 ch, ss in first ch to form a ring.

Round 1 3 ch, 2 tr in ring, *2 ch, 3 tr in ring, rep from * twice more, 2 ch, ss in top of 3-ch to join. Fasten off yarn A.

Round 2 Join yarn B in any centre tr from 3-tr group on prev round. 3 ch, *1 tr in each tr to corner sp, (2 tr, 4 ch, 2 tr) in next 2-ch corner sp; rep from * to end, 1 tr in each rem tr, ss in top of 3-ch to join. (7 tr on each side of square)

Round 3 3 ch, *1 tr in each tr to corner, (2 tr, 4 ch, 2 tr) in 4-ch corner sp; rep from * to end, 1 tr in each rem tr, ss in top of 3-ch to join. (11 tr on each side of square)

Fasten off yarn B.

Round 4 Join yarn A in any tr st. Rep round 3 with yarn A. (15 tr on each side of square)

Fasten off yarn A.

Make 27 more squares using yarn B in rounds 2 and 3 (28 squares total), and 28 squares using yarn C in rounds 2 and 3.

Join Squares

Place two squares wrong sides together. Work dc seam in back loops only of each st. Join squares into strips of 8 squares. Lay two strips of 8 with wrong sides together. Work dc join in back loops only of each st. Continue until all squares are joined.

Edging

Round 1 Join yarn A in any tr. 3 ch, *1 tr in each tr to corner sp, (2 tr, 4 ch, 2 tr) into each 4-ch corner sp; rep from * around entire blanket, 1 tr in each rem tr, ss in top of 3-ch to join.

Round 2 Rep round 1.

Fasten off. Weave in all ends.

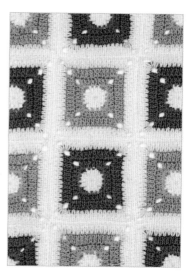

Seams

The blanket squares are joined by working through only the back loops of each stitch. This helps the blanket to lie flat.

Colour

Squares are arranged here in alternating colours, using 28 squares of each colour to form seven rows of eight squares.

How to **Crochet Edgings**

Edgings add a neat finish to your work and can helpfully disguise untidy edges. Double crochet edgings provide a simple, narrow border, but pay particular attention to the row-end sides of the crochet. More ornate borders can either be made separately or crocheted onto the work.

Double crochet edging

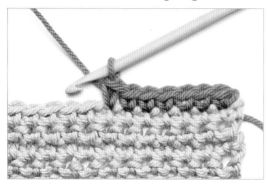

Row ends are more uneven than top edges

ALONG TOP OR BOTTOM OF A ROW
To work double crochet along the top or bottom edge, join the yarn to the first stitch with a slip stitch, work 1 ch, 1 dc in the same place as the slip stitch, then work 1 dc in each stitch all along the edge.

ALONG ROW ENDS
It is not as easy to achieve an even edging along the row ends and you may need to make adjustments. If the finished edging looks flared, try working fewer stitches per row-end; if it looks puckered, try working more stitches.

Sewing on edgings

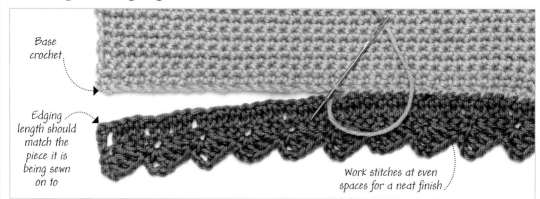

Base crochet

Edging length should match the piece it is being sewn on to

Work stitches at even spaces for a neat finish

Sew the edging in place with a yarn that matches the base crochet and a blunt-ended yarn needle. Secure the yarn at the end of the seam with 2 or 3 overcast stitches. Then work evenly spaced overcast stitches through both the base crochet and the edging, as shown.

Crocheting edging directly onto edge

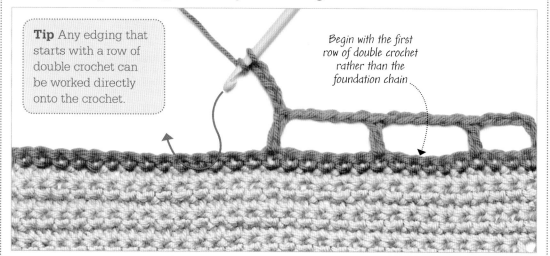

Tip Any edging that starts with a row of double crochet can be worked directly onto the crochet.

Begin with the first row of double crochet rather than the foundation chain

1 As you won't be making a foundation chain, choose an edging pattern that will work with the number of stitches on the base crochet. Start by working a row of double crochet onto the base crochet. Then turn and work the next row of the edging pattern.

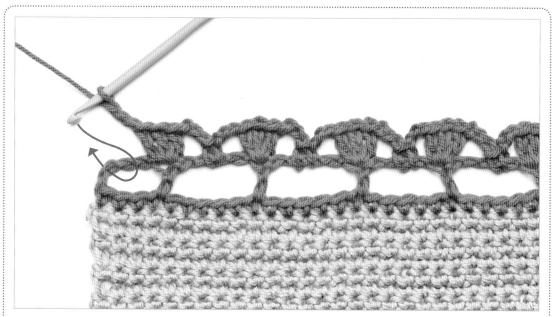

2 At the end of the second row, turn the crochet in the usual manner and work the remaining rows of the edging as described in your pattern. (The third and final row of the Simple Shell Edging on p.172 is being worked in this example.)

Gallery of **Simple Edging Patterns**

A decorative crochet edging can transform an otherwise plain item.
All the patterns that follow are worked widthwise, so make a foundation
chain roughly equivalent to the length of edging you need, allowing
extra if there are corners to wrap around. Try these edgings on towel
ends, throws, baby blankets, necklines, and cuffs.

Double Loop Edging

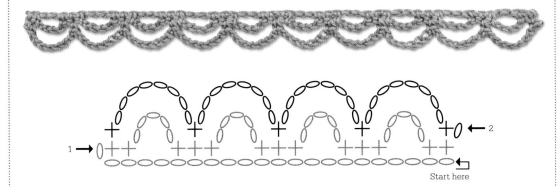

Make a multiple of 5 ch, plus 2 extra.
Row 1 (WS) 1 dc in 2nd ch from hook, 1 dc in next ch, *5 ch, miss next 2 ch, 1 dc in each of next 3 ch; rep from * to last 4 ch, 5 ch, miss next 2 ch, 1 dc in each of last 2 ch, turn.

Row 2 1 ch, 1 dc in first dc, *8 ch, 1 dc in centre dc of next group of 3-dc (at other side of 5-ch loop); rep from * working last dc in last dc of row 1.
Fasten off, weave in ends.

Picot Scallop Edging

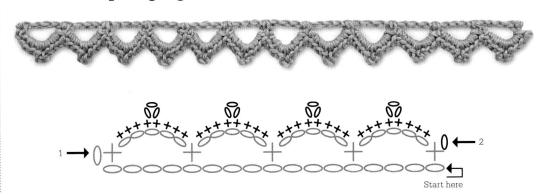

Make a multiple of 4 ch, plus 2 extra.
Row 1 (WS) 1 dc in 2nd ch from hook, *5 ch, miss next 3 ch, 1 dc in next ch; rep from * to end, turn.

Row 2 1 ch, *(4 dc, 3 ch, 4 dc) in next 5-ch loop; rep from * to end.
Fasten off, weave in ends.

Triple Picot Edging

Make a multiple of 6 ch, plus 2 extra.
Row 1 (WS) 1 dc in 2nd ch from hook, 1 dc in each of rem ch, turn.
Row 2 5 ch, (1 dc, [5 ch, 1 dc] twice) in first dc, *4 ch, miss next 5 dc, (1 dc, [5 ch, 1 dc] 3 times) in next dc; rep from * to end.
Fasten off, weave in ends.

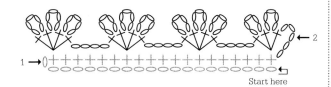

Pillar Edging

Make a multiple of 10 ch, plus 2 extra.
Row 1 (WS) 1 dc in 2nd ch from hook, 1 dc in each of rem ch, turn.
Row 2 1 ch, 1 dc in first dc, *2 ch, miss next dc, 1 tr in next dc, (2 ch, miss next dc, 1 dtr in next dc) twice, 2 ch, miss next dc, 1 tr in next dc, 2 ch, miss next dc, 1 dc in next dc; rep from * to end.
Fasten off, weave in ends.

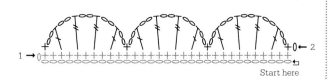

Step Edging

Make a multiple of 4 ch, plus 3 extra.
Row 1 (WS) 1 tr in 4th ch from hook, 1 tr in each of rem ch, turn.
Row 2 3 ch, 3 tr in first tr, *miss next 3 tr, (1 dc, 3 ch, 3 tr) in next tr; rep from * to last 3 tr, miss last 3 tr, 1 dc in top of 3-ch at end.
Fasten off, weave in ends.

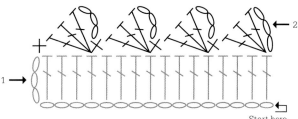

Simple Shell Edging

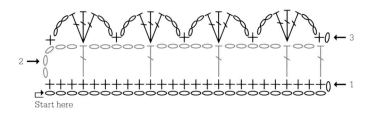

Start here

Make a multiple of 6 ch, plus 2 extra.
Row 1 (RS) 1 dc in 2nd ch from hook, 1 dc in each of rem ch, turn.
Row 2 5 ch, miss first 3 dc, 1 tr in next dc, *5 ch, miss next 5 dc, 1 tr in next dc; rep from * to last 3 dc, 2 ch, miss next 2 dc, 1 tr in last dc, turn.

Row 3 1 ch, 1 dc in first tr, 3 ch, 3 tr in next tr, *3 ch, 1 dc in next 5-ch space, 3 ch, 3 tr in next tr; rep from *, ending with 3 ch, miss first 2 ch of last 5-ch, 1 dc in next ch.
Fasten off, weave in ends.

Cluster Scallop Edging

Start here

Make a multiple of 8 ch, plus 2 extra.
Row 1 (RS) 1 dc in 2nd ch from hook, 1 dc in each of rem ch, turn.
Row 2 1 ch, 1 dc in first dc, 1 dc in each of next 2 dc, *6 ch, miss next 3 dc, 1 dc in each of next 5 dc; rep from * to last 6 dc, 6 ch, miss next 3 dc, 1 dc in each of last 3 dc, turn.
Row 3 3 ch, (yrh, insert hook in ch sp, yrh and draw a loop through, yrh and draw through first 2 loops on hook) 3 times in next 6-ch sp, yrh and draw through all 4 loops

on hook to close 3-tr group (called 3-tr cluster), *4 ch, 3-tr cluster in same ch sp, 4 ch, 3-tr cluster in same ch sp but do not close cluster (leave last 4 loops on hook), 3-tr cluster in next 6-ch sp and close this cluster and previous cluster at the same time by drawing a loop through all 7 loops on hook; rep from * to last 6-ch sp, (4 ch, 3-tr cluster in same ch sp) twice, 1 tr in last dc of row 2.
Fasten off, weave in ends.

Chain Fringe

Note: This fringe is worked into a row of dc. The depth of the fringe can be altered by changing the number of chains in each fringe loop. To start the edging, make 1 ch more than the required number of dc.

Row 1 (WS) 1 dc in 2nd ch from hook, 1 dc in each of rem ch, turn.

Row 2 1 ch, 1 dc in first dc, 29 ch, 1 dc in same place as last dc, *1 dc in next dc, 29 ch, 1 dc in same place as last dc; rep from * to end.

Fasten off, weave in ends.

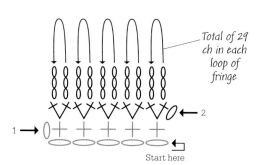

Total of 29 ch in each loop of fringe

Start here

Twirl Fringe

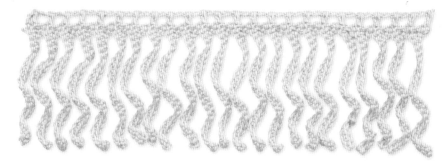

Note: The fringe will twirl naturally; do not press out the twirls.

To start edging, make a multiple of 2 ch.

Row 1 (WS) 1 dtr in 4th ch from hook, *1 ch, miss next ch, 1 dtr in next ch; rep from * to end, turn.

Row 2 1 ch, 1 dc in first dtr, *24 ch, 1 dc in 2nd ch from hook, 1 dc in each of rem 22 ch, 1 dc in next dtr; rep from * to end.

Fasten off, weave in ends.

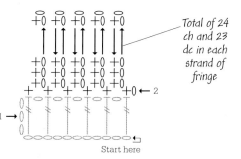

Total of 24 ch and 23 dc in each strand of fringe

Start here

How to **Work Step Decreases**

The shaping techniques that you have learned so far enable you to
either narrow or widen the rows gradually. Step decreases and increases
expand your options: you can use them to create bolder shaping by
forming "steps" at the edges of the crochet. The Baby's Cardigan project
(see p.178) uses step decreases to form the neckline.

First dc of
repositioned row

Slip stitch to
correct position

AT BEGINNING OF ROW

Slip stitches can be used to make a step
decrease that moves the starting point of the
new row inwards. As the example above
shows, to decrease 3 stitches at the beginning
of a row of double crochet, work 1 chain and
then 1 slip stitch into each of the first 4
dc. Next, work 1 chain, then work the first
dc in the same place that the last slip stitch
was worked. Continue along the row in the
usual way.

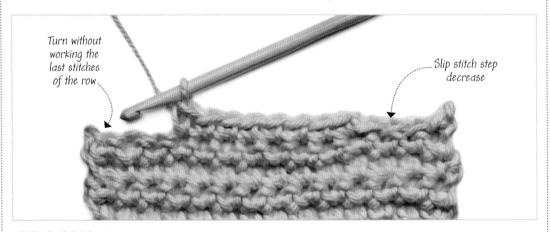

Turn without
working the
last stitches
of the row

Slip stitch step
decrease

AT END OF ROW

For a 3-stitch step decrease at the end of the
row, simply work up to the last 3 stitches at
the end of the row and turn, leaving the last
3 stitches unworked. These two techniques
for making step decreases at either end of a
row can be used for all crochet stitches.

How to **Work Step Increases**

Step increases allow you to extend the width of your crochet piece by several stitches from one row to the next. The "step" creates a sharp angle, which looks neat when you are adding integrated bag handles, garment sleeves, and more. Different techniques are needed on each side of the row, so see page 176 for step increases at the end of rows.

Step increase at the beginning of a row

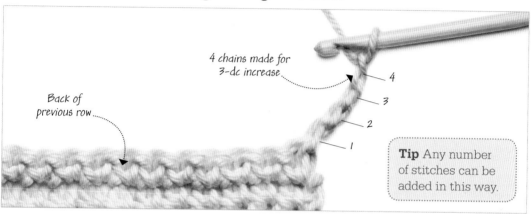

4 chains made for 3-dc increase

Back of previous row

4
3
2
1

Tip Any number of stitches can be added in this way.

1 A step increase at the beginning of a row moves the starting point of the new row outwards. As the example above shows, to add a 3-stitch step increase at the beginning of a row of double crochet, begin by making 4 chains as shown here. (Always make one chain more than the number of extra double crochets required, as a turning chain.)

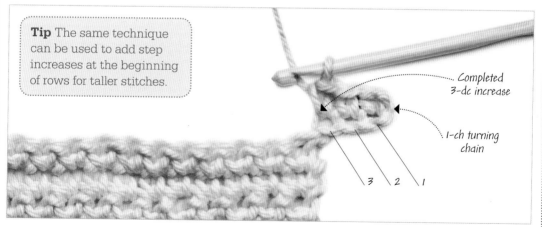

Tip The same technique can be used to add step increases at the beginning of rows for taller stitches.

Completed 3-dc increase

1-ch turning chain

3 2 1

2 Work the first dc into the second chain from the hook. Then work 1 dc into each of the remaining 2 chains. This creates a 3-dc increase at the beginning of the row. Continue the row in the usual way, working 1 dc into each dc in the row below.

Step increase at the end of a row

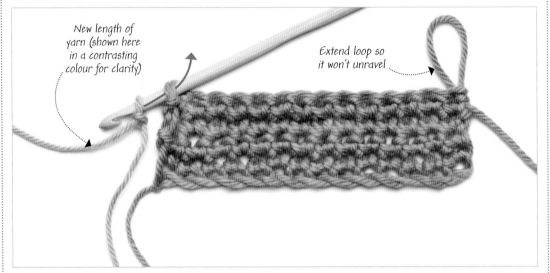

New length of yarn (shown here in a contrasting colour for clarity)

Extend loop so it won't unravel

1 Before starting the row with the step increase at the end, remove the hook from the loop at the beginning of the row. Extend the working loop to stop it from unravelling.

Then, using a short length of matching yarn, place a slip knot on the hook and draw this loop through the last stitch at the end of the row, where you'll be making the increase.

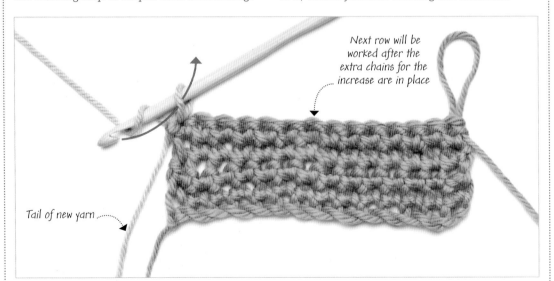

Next row will be worked after the extra chains for the increase are in place

Tail of new yarn

2 There is now one loop on the hook – this forms the first extra chain at the end of the row. Continue making chains until you have made as many as the required number of

extra stitches. The added chains create a pathway for the step increase, providing somewhere to make the new stitches of the increase when the next row is worked.

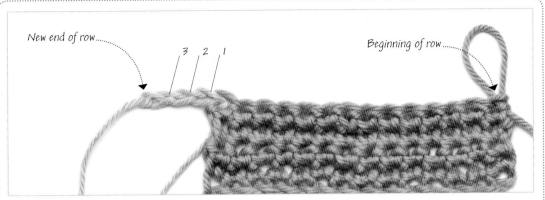

3 The step increase can be as long or as short as required. For a 3-stitch step increase, make a total of 3 chains. Then fasten off (weave in the new yarn tails later).

4 Return to the beginning of the row, slip the loop back onto the hook and tighten it, then work to the end of the row in the usual way until you reach the added chains.

5 Work 1 dc into each of the 3 added chains. This creates a 3-dc increase. The same technique can be used to make step increases for taller stitches too.

Make a Baby's Cardigan

This beautiful cardigan is sure to keep your little one warm and cosy. The simple construction cleverly uses step increases to incorporate the sleeves into the body of the cardigan, so very little seaming is required.

Instructions

Yarn

You can use any DK wool or wool blend yarn. Here we have used Jarol Heritage DK 100g (250m/273yd) in 2 colours

A: 137 Lime x 2 balls
B: 100 Cream x 1 ball

Hook Size

4mm hook

Notions

10mm (½in) buttons x 3

Tension

17 htr to 10cm (4in)

Size

To fit a baby aged 0–6 (6–12) months

Special Notes

The pattern is given for two sizes. For a baby aged 0–6 months, follow the first set of instructions throughout; for a baby aged 6–12 months, follow the instructions given in brackets.

Pattern

Front (make 2)

With yarn B, make 22 (25) ch.
Row 1 1 htr into 3rd ch from hook, 1 htr into each ch to end, turn. 20 (23) sts
Row 2 2 ch (counts as 1 htr), 1 htr into each st to end, turn.
Change to yarn A and work in rows of htr until piece measures 15 (16)cm/6 (6½)in.
Next row: 27 (32) ch, 1 htr into 3rd ch from hook, 1 htr into each ch to end of ch. 25 (30) sts increased for arm. Work across body stitches. 45 (53) htr. Work in rows of htr on these sts until piece measures approx 20 (21)cm/8 (8½)in from hem, ending at arm edge.

137 Lime x 2   **100 Cream x 1**

4mm hook

Next row: Work in htr to last 6 (8) sts, 1 dc into next st, turn, leaving rem sts unworked for neck opening.
Next row: Ss into each of first 5 sts, 1 htr in each st to end of row. Work in rows of htr until piece measures 24 (25)cm/9½ (10)in to shoulder.
Fasten off yarn.

Back

With yarn B, make 43 (47) ch.
Row 1 1 htr into 3rd ch from hook, 1 htr into each ch to end, turn. 41 (45) sts
Row 2 2 ch (counts as 1 htr), 1 htr into each st, turn.
Change to yarn A and work in rows of htr until piece measures the same as front to one row below armhole.
At end of row, work 25 (30) ch, fasten off yarn.
Rejoin yarn to opposite row end, work 27 (32) ch, turn.
Next row: 1 htr into 3rd ch from hook, 1 htr into each ch to end of ch. 25 (30) sts increased for arm. Work in htr across body stitches, then 1 htr into each ch to end for opposite arm. 91 (105) sts
Work in rows of htr on these sts until piece measures same as front to one row below shoulder.
Next row: Work in htr across 35 (40) sts. Fasten off yarn, leaving rem sts unworked.
Rejoin yarn to opposite arm edge, work in htr across 35 (40) sts, fasten off yarn, leaving rem 21 (25) sts unworked for neck.

Border and Neck Edge

Rejoin yarn A to bottom of right front edge and work evenly in dc up edge, then round neck. At top of left edge, work 5 ch for button loop, then work 4 dc down edge, 5 ch, 4 dc, 5 ch, dc to bottom of left front. Sew buttons to right front, corresponding to the button loops.

Finishing

Block all pieces lightly to shape. Sew shoulder seams, then sew up each underarm and side seam. Finish with the contrast border on the cuffs.

Cuffs

With yarn B, rejoin yarn to cuff and work 2 rows of dc evenly all round the edge.
Weave in all ends.

Sleeves

Extra chain stitches are added to crochet the sleeves directly onto the body piece (see step increases, pp.175–77).

Sleeves are made as a part of the back and front pieces of the cardigan

Neckline

To decrease and shape the neck opening, slip stitches are used for some rows, while some stitches are left unworked (see step decreases, p.174).

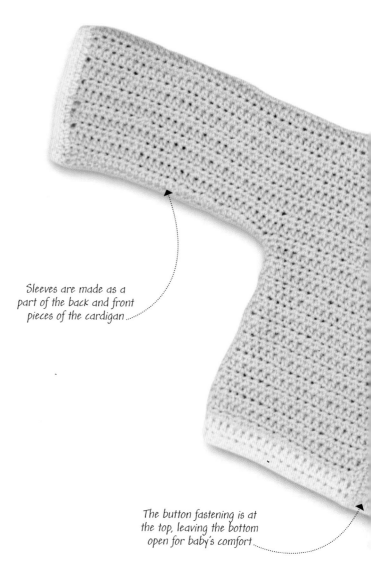

The button fastening is at the top, leaving the bottom open for baby's comfort

Tip By clever uses of simple increases and decreases, this pattern creates a cardigan with integrated sleeves, so there are only three pieces to sew together at the end. To make sure you understand this method, read carefully through the pattern and check the instructions for step increases and decreases on pages 174–177 before you embark on this project.

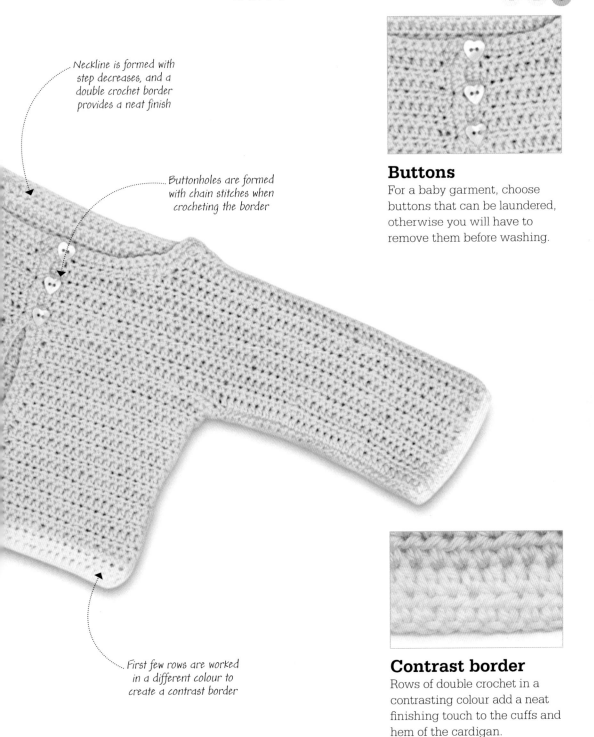

Neckline is formed with
step decreases, and a
double crochet border
provides a neat finish

Buttonholes are formed
with chain stitches when
crocheting the border

Buttons

For a baby garment, choose
buttons that can be laundered,
otherwise you will have to
remove them before washing.

First few rows are worked
in a different colour to
create a contrast border

Contrast border

Rows of double crochet in a
contrasting colour add a neat
finishing touch to the cuffs and
hem of the cardigan.

Make a Teddy Bear

This cute little teddy is the perfect companion for an older baby. Made in continuous rounds, the head is started from the top and the body from the bottom. The two pieces are then stuffed and joined, and arms, legs, and ears are made separately and sewn in place.

Instructions

Yarn

You can use any DK weight yarn. Here we have used Stylecraft Special DK 100g (295m/323yd):

Teddy

1003 Aster x 1 ball

Scarf

1005 Cream x 1 ball

1003 Aster x 1

1005 Cream x 1

Size

15cm (6in)

Hook Size

A: 3mm hook (for teddy)

B: 4mm hook (for scarf)

3mm hook

4mm hook

Notions

Stitch marker

Toy stuffing

Embroidery thread in light brown and black

Pattern

Head

Work 6 dc into a magic adjustable ring (see p.78). Pull tail to close.

Round 1 2 dc in each dc to end. (12sts)

Round 2 *1 dc in next dc, 2 dc in next dc; rep from * to end. (18sts)

Round 3 *1 dc in each of next 2 dc, 2 dc in next dc; rep from * to end. (24sts)

Round 4 *1 dc in each of next 3 dc, 2 dc in next dc; rep from * to end. (30sts)

Round 5 *1 dc in each of next 4 dc, 2 dc in next dc; rep from * to end. (36sts)

Round 6 *1 dc in each of next 5 dc, 2 dc in next dc; rep from * to end. (42sts)

Rounds 7–14 1 dc in each dc to end. (42sts)

Round 15 *1 dc in each of next 5 dc, dc2tog; rep from * to end. (36sts)

Round 16 *1 dc in each of next 4 dc, dc2tog; rep from * to end. (30sts)

Round 17 *1 dc in each of next 3 dc, dc2tog; rep from * to end. (24sts)

Fasten off, leaving a long tail. Stuff firmly, but leave open for the moment. (Embroider eyes, nose, and mouth after assembling.)

Ears (make 2)

Work 5 dc into a magic adjustable ring. Pull tail to close.

Round 1 2 dc in each dc to end. (10sts)

Rounds 2–3 1 dc in each dc to end. (10sts)

Fasten off, leaving a long tail. Use tail to sew open ends of ears to head.

Body

Work 6 dc into a magic adjustable ring. Pull tail to close.

Round 1 2 dc in each dc to end. (12sts)

Round 2 *1 dc in next dc, 2 dc in next dc; rep from * to end. (18sts)

Round 3 *1 dc in each of next 2 dc, 2 dc in next dc; rep from * to end. (24sts)

Round 4 *1 dc in each of next 3 dc, 2 dc in next dc; rep from * to end. (30sts)

Round 5 *1 dc in each of next 4 dc, 2 dc in next dc; rep from * to end. (36sts)

Round 6 *1 dc in each of next 5 dc, 2 dc in next dc; rep from * to end. (42sts)

Rounds 7–14 1 dc in each dc to end. (42sts)

Round 15 *1 dc in each of next 5 dc, dc2tog; rep from * to end. (36sts)

Rounds 16–17 1 dc in each dc to end. (36sts)

Round 18 *1 dc in each of next 4 dc, dc2tog; rep from * to end. (30sts)

Rounds 19–20 1 dc in each dc to end. (30sts)

Round 21 *1 dc in each of next 3 dc, dc2tog; rep from * to end. (24sts)

Rounds 22–23 1 dc in each dc to end. (24sts)

Fasten off, leaving a long tail. Stuff firmly. Sew body to head.

Legs (make 2)

Work 6 dc into a magic adjustable ring. Pull tail to close.

Round 1 2 dc in each dc to end. (12sts)

Round 2 *1 dc in next dc, 2 dc in next dc; rep from * to end. (18sts)

183

Round 3 *1 dc in each of next 2 dc, 2 dc in next dc; rep from * to end. (24sts)
Round 4 *1 dc in each of next 3 dc, 2 dc in next dc; rep from * to end. (30sts)
Round 5 dc2tog to end. (15sts)
Rounds 6–9 1 dc in each dc to end. (15sts)
Fasten off, leaving a long tail. Stuff firmly, use tail to sew legs to body.

Arms (make 2)
Work 6 dc into a magic adjustable ring. Pull tail to close.

Round 1 2 dc in each dc to end. (12sts)
Rounds 2–8 1 dc in each dc to end. (12sts)
Fasten off, leaving a long tail. Stuff firmly, use tail to sew arms to body.

Scarf
Make 31 ch.
Row 1 Miss 1 dc, 1 dc in each of rem 30 chs. (30sts)
Row 2 1 ch, 1 dc in each dc to end.
Fasten off, weave in ends.

Tip Each part of the teddy – head, body, ears, arms, and legs – is made in the round. Each piece is made in a spiral, with no joins at the end of each round and no turning chain. To keep track of rounds, use a stitch marker in the first stitch of every round.

Tie the scarf around the bear's neck (omit the scarf for small babies)

Stuffing and assembling toy pieces

1 Use a blunt tool – such as the handle of your crochet hook – to push stuffing into the open end of the body, head, arm, and leg pieces; do not overstuff.

2 Pin the smaller pieces to the body one at a time. Thread the long yarn tail into a blunt-ended yarn needle and stitch edges onto the body.

Stuff legs firmly, but not so much that the shape will distort

Tip Be careful to remove all pins before giving the teddy to a child. Use large-headed pins so that they don't accidently get lost in the crocheted pieces.

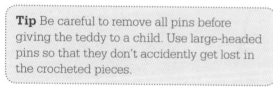

Embroider facial features after
stuffing and assembling

Stitch open edge
of ear firmly to
the head

Head and neck

The head and neck are both
worked to the same number of
stitches, and are attached to
each other with matching yarn.

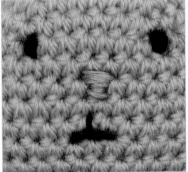

Face

The teddy's eyes, nose, and
mouth are embroidered on the
finished head with black and
light brown embroidery thread.

Make Baby's Shoes

These adorable little shoes are made to fit a newborn baby; crossover straps help to keep the shoes in place. The shoes are made in the round, starting with the sole. Use the softest yarn to protect your baby's delicate skin.

Instructions

Yarn

You can use any DK wool or wool blend yarn. Here we have used Sublime Baby Cashmere Merino Silk DK 50g (116m/127yd) 002 Cuddle x 1 ball

Hook Size

4mm hook

Notions

Stitch marker
Small buttons x 4

Tension

Measure tension after completing the sole of each shoe. The length of the sole should be at least 8.5cm (3¼in)

Size

To fit a newborn baby

Pattern

Shoes (make 2)

Make 9 ch.
Round 1 Miss 1 ch, 1 dc in each ch to end, 4 dc in last ch. Working down other side of foundation ch, 1 dc in each ch to end, 4 dc in last ch. (22sts)
Round 2 *1 dc in each of next 7 sts, (1 dc in next st, 2 dc in next st) twice; rep from * once more. (26sts)
Round 3 *1 dc in each of next 7 sts, (1 dc in each of next 2 sts, 2 dc in next st) twice; rep from * once more. (30sts)
Round 4 *1 dc in each of next 7 sts, (1 dc in each of next 3 sts, 2 dc in next st) twice; rep from * once more. (34sts)
Round 5 Working into back loops only, 1 dc in each dc to end. (34sts)
Round 6 1 dc in each of next 7 sts, (1 dc in each of next 3 sts, dc2tog) twice, 1 dc in each of

002 Cuddle x 1

4mm hook

next 17 sts. (32sts)
Round 7 1 dc in each of next 7 sts, tr2tog 4 times, 1 dc in each of next 7 sts, 1 htr in each of next 10 sts. (28sts)
Round 8 1 dc in each of next 7 sts, tr2tog twice, 1 dc in each of next 7 sts, 1 htr in each of next 10 sts, ss in first st to close. (26sts)
Do not fasten off yarn.

First strap: 9 ch, 1 dc in 4th ch from hook, 1 dc in each of next 5 ch, ss in 1st st. Fasten off.
Second strap: Rejoin yarn on other side of shoe at corresponding st (the last dc before the htr sts) and rep instructions for first strap. Fasten off, weave in ends.
Attach buttons securely, as shown in picture.

Sole

Each sole is worked in rounds without joining. Use a stitch marker throughout to mark the first stitch of every round.

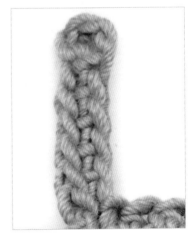

Button loop

The button loop at the end of each strap needs to fit snugly around the button. Adjust the size, if necessary, by adding or subtracting chains.

Index

About the Author

Susie Johns studied Fine Art at the Slade school in London, before working as a magazine and partworks editor for 11 years, specializing in cookery and crafts. She has since written and illustrated books on a variety of creative subjects, including knitting, crochet, embroidery, and papercrafts, and has had features and interviews published in a wide range of magazines.

As a crochet designer, Susie's creative skills are in great demand, not only for making garments and accessories but also novelty crochet items such as fruits, vegetables, flowers, animals, birds, dolls, mascots, and puppets.

Susie teaches drawing and painting at an adult education college in Greenwich, London, and runs workshops in knitting, crochet, and customizing clothes. She is the founder member of "Knitting Night at The Pelton", a weekly drop-in group.

Acknowledgments

Photographic Credits

The publishers would to thank Ruth Jenkinson for new photography, and her assistant Julie Stewart.
All images © Dorling Kindersley.
For further information see
www.dkimages.com

Publisher's Acknowledgments

Many people have helped in the making of this book. Special thanks are due to the crochet designers who created the projects in this book:

Susie Johns designed the Washcloth, Phone Cover, Cafetière Cosy, Towel Edging, Friendship Bracelets, and Tote Bag projects.
Catherine Hirst designed the Toy Balls, Project Basket, Bookmark, Clutch Bag, Ribbed Scarf, Lacy Scarf, String Bag, Teddy Bear, and Baby's Shoes projects.
Claire Montgomerie designed the Round Cushion, Chevron Cushion, Baby's Hat, and Baby's Cardigan projects.
Erin McCarthy designed the Patchwork Blanket project.

Many thanks are also due to **Sally Harding**, who wrote the original technique sequences and equipment information.

The yarn weight symbols and corresponding categories on page 17 have been devised by the Craft Yarn Council of America (YarnStandards.com).

Dorling Kindersley would also like to thank:

In the UK
Editorial assistance and proofreading May Corfield
Indexer Jane Coulter

In India
Proofreading Charis Bhagianathan
Design assistance Sourabh Challariya